TEACHIN
SECOND-LANC
WRITING: INTERACTING
WITH TEXT

Cherry Campbell

Monterey Institute of International Studies

A TeacherSource Book

Donald Freeman
Series Editor

Heinle & Heinle Publishers
I⟨T⟩P An International Thomson Publishing Company

Pacific Grove • Albany • Bonn • Boston • Cincinnati • Detroit • London
Madrid • Melbourne • Mexico City • New York • Paris
San Francisco • Tokyo • Toronto • Washington

The publication of *Teaching Second-Language Writing: Interacting with Text*
was directed by members of the Newbury House ESL/EFL
Team at Heinle & Heinle:

Erik Gundersen, Editorial Director
Jonathan Boggs, Marketing Director
Kristin M. Thalheimer, Senior Production Services Coordinator
Thomas Healy, Developmental Editor
Stanley J. Galek, Vice President and Publisher/ESL

Also participating in the publication of this program were:

Designer: Jessica Robison
Project Management and Composition: Imageset
Manufacturing Coordinator: Mary Beth Hennebury
Associate Market Development Director: Mary Sutton
Cover Designer: Ha D. Nguyen

Heinle & Heinle is a division of International Thomson Publishing, Inc.

Manufactured in Canada

The author and publisher are grateful for permission to reprint specific material on the following pages:

pp. 37. From LOST IN TRANSLATION by Eva Hoffman, copyright © 1989 by
Eva Hoffman. Used by permission of Dutton Signet, a division of Penguin Books USA Inc.,
and William Heinemann.

pp. 38. From AMANDA BARKER from SPOON RIVER ANTHOLOGY by Edgar Lee Masters
© 1962. Originally published by Macmillan Co. Used by permission of Hilary Masters.

pp. 41-2. From ROAD SCHOLAR: Coast to Coast Late in the Century by Andrei Codrescu.
Text copyright © 1993 Andrei Codrescu. Reprinted with permission of Hyperion.

ISBN 0-8384-7892-1

10 9 8 7 6 5 4 3 2 1

TABLE OF CONTENTS

Thank You

The series editor, authors and publisher would like to thank the following individuals who offered many helpful insights throughout the development of the **TeacherSource** series.

Linda Lonon Blanton	University of New Orleans
Tommie Brasel	New Mexico School for the Deaf
Jill Burton	University of South Australia
Margaret B. Cassidy	Brattleboro Union High School, Vermont
Florence Decker	University of Texas at El Paso
Silvia G. Diaz	Dade County Public Schools, Florida
Margo Downey	Boston University
Alvino Fantini	School for International Training
Sandra Fradd	University of Miami
Jerry Gebhard	Indiana University of Pennsylvania
Fred Genesee	University of California at Davis
Stacy Gildenston	Colorado State University
Jeannette Gordon	Illinois Resource Center
Else Hamayan	Illinois Resource Center
Sarah Hudelson	Arizona State University
Joan Jamieson	Northern Arizona University
Elliot L. Judd	University of Illinois at Chicago
Donald N. Larson	Bethel College, Minnesota (Emeritus)
Numa Markee	University of Illinois at Urbana Champaign
Denise E. Murray	San Jose State University
Meredith Pike-Baky	University of California at Berkeley
Sara L. Sanders	Coastal Carolina University
Lilia Savova	Indiana University of Pennsylvania
Donna Sievers	Garden Grove Unified School District, California
Ruth Spack	Tufts University
Leo van Lier	Monterey Institute of International Studies

For Doc,
forever

ACKNOWLEDGMENTS

Until the summer of 1997 I had never become either a bride or a book author. The wedding ceremony, celebration, and honeymoon took place while the book manuscript was out for review. Both came to pass, less because of my doing than because of what other people brought to me. Before I met my husband, life was just fine. My life was a simple tune. Now, to borrow the sentiment from Phoebe Snow, my husband is the melody that makes my life a song. I am blessed.

And what could be finer than to call on favorite colleagues to help you write a book? In the following pages you'll hear the stories of Kim, June, and other students I've worked with and learned from. Also, what excites me most, you'll hear classroom stories from five great writing instructors, Ron Balsamo, KimMarie Cole, Melinda Erickson, Rona Nashiro Koe, and Amy Tickle, who continue to teach me along with their ESL writing students. To collaborate with all of them, I am truly blessed.

Thank you to Erik Gundersen and Donald Freeman for the series, the opportunity, and the encouragement. Donald, I offer you high praise that I have learned from students at my school: you are honest and kind. Thank you to my reviewers for the audience. Thank you to Thomas Healy, Kristin Thalheimer, Mary Reed, Jessica Robison, Su Wilson, Mark Gerardi, and Talbot Hamlin for their skilled work. Thank you to the Center for Language Education and Research and to the National Council of Teachers of English for partial funding of my dissertation research. To my Monterey family: thanks to Kathi Bailey for the nudge; thanks to Ruth Larimer for the leave; thanks to Jean Turner for keeping me calm; thanks to Lynn Goldstein and to six years' worth of English Studies instructors for talking to me about teaching writing; likewise, thanks to Gary Buck, Martha Clark Cummings, John Hedgcock, Peter Shaw, Michaele Smith, Marya Teutsch-Dwyer, Leo van Lier, Devon Woods, and students from my teaching of writing courses; thanks to Alayne Cramer and Paul Magnuson for all that feedback; and thanks to my ESL Content Writing students for smiling and nodding when I spoke of pinball. Thank you, Esther, for the daily supervision.

Most of all, to my cohorts in teaching narratives and nuptials: my wholehearted thanks go to Melinda, Amy, KimMarie, Rona, and Ron. And, Doc, my wholehearted thanks will never be enough. Instead, I give you my whole heart.

PREFACE

Driving just south of White River Junction, the snow had started falling in earnest. The light was flat, although it was mid-morning, making it almost impossible to distinguish the highway in the gray-white swirling snow. I turned on the radio, partly as a distraction and partly to help me concentrate on the road ahead; the announcer was talking about the snow. "The state highway department advises motorists to use extreme caution and to drive with their headlights to ensure maximum visibility." He went on, his tone shifting slightly, "Ray Burke, the state highway supervisor, just called to say that one of the plows almost hit a car just south of Exit 6 because the person driving hadn't turned on his lights. He really wants people to put their headlights on because it is very tough to see in this stuff." I checked, almost reflexively, to be sure that my headlights were on, as I drove into the churning snow.

How can information serve those who hear or read it in making sense of their own worlds? How can it enable them to reason about what they do and to take appropriate actions based on that reasoning? My experience with the radio in the snow storm illustrates two different ways of providing the same message: the need to use your headlights when you drive in heavy snow. The first offers dispassionate information; the second tells the same content in a personal, compelling story. The first disguises its point of view; the second explicitly grounds the general information in a particular time and place. Each means of giving information has its role, but I believe the second is ultimately more useful in helping people make sense of what they are doing. When I heard Ray Burke's story about the plow, I made sure my headlights were on.

In what is written about teaching, it is rare to find accounts in which the author's experience and point of view are central. A point of view is not simply an opinion; neither is it a whimsical or impressionistic claim. Rather, a point of view lays out what the author thinks and why; to borrow the phrase from writing teacher Natalie Goldberg, "it sets down the bones." The problem is that much of what is available in professional development in language-teacher education concentrates on telling rather than on point of view. The telling is prescriptive, like the radio announcer's first statement. It emphasizes what is important to know and do, what is current in theory and research, and therefore what you—as a practicing teacher—should do. But this telling disguises the teller; it hides the point of view that can enable you to make sense of what is told.

The **TeacherSource** series offers you a point of view on second/foreign language teaching. Each author in this series has had to lay out what she or he believes is central to the topic, and how she or he has come to this understanding. So as a reader, you will find this book has a personality; it is not anonymous. It comes as a story, not as a directive, and it is meant to create a relationship with you rather than assume your attention. As a practitioner, its point of view can help you in your own work by providing a sounding board for your ideas and a metric for your own thinking. It can suggest courses of action and explain why these make sense to the author. And you can take from it what you will, and do with it what you can. This book will not tell you what to think; it is meant to help you make sense of what you do.

The point of view in **TeacherSource** is built out of three strands: **Teachers' Voices**, **Frameworks**, and **Investigations**. Each author draws together these strands uniquely, as suits his or her topic and more crucially his or her point of view. All materials in TeacherSource have these three strands. The **Teachers' Voices** are practicing language teachers from various settings who tell about their experience of the topic. The **Frameworks** lay out what the author believes is important to know about his or her topic and its key concepts and issues. These fundamentals define the area of language teaching and learning about which she or he is writing. The **Investigations** are meant to engage you, the reader, in relating the topic to your own teaching, students, and classroom. They are activities which you can do alone or with colleagues, to reflect on teaching and learning and/or try out ideas in practice.

Each strand offers a point of view on the book's topic. The **Teachers' Voices** relate the points of view of various practitioners; the **Frameworks** establish the point of view of the professional community; and the **Investigations** invite you to develop your own point of view, through experience with reference to your setting. Together these strands should serve in making sense of the topic.

In her book, *Teaching Second-Language Writing: Interacting with Text*, Cherry Campbell examines how writing can integrate with other areas of second-language use both in and beyond the classroom. She believes, as she says in her Introduction, that "teaching second-language writing has become an important responsibility of school systems with growing immigrant populations." For this reason, she has chosen to focus the book on students who are learning to write in grades from middle school through university in the United States. The insights and lessons she describes are applicable well beyond these complex environments, however. For Campbell, to teach writing is to enable students to navigate its game, a game that is at once rule-governed, skill-based, and many times beyond the writer's direct manipulation or control. Situating her comments firmly within her own growing up as a student and teacher of writing, Campbell also draws from the experiences of other teachers to elaborate key conceptual questions. Thus Campbell moves beyond the distinction often made between teaching writing as a process or a product, to view writing as a situated practice in which student and teacher navigate conventions to create and express meaning.

This book, like all elements of the **TeacherSource** series, is intended to serve you in understanding your work as a language teacher. It may lead you to thinking about what you do in different ways and/or to taking specific actions in your teaching. Or it may do neither. But we intend, through the variety of points of view presented in this fashion, to offer you access to choices in teaching that you may not have thought of before and thus to help your teaching make more sense.

—*Donald Freeman, Series Editor*

Introduction

Teaching second-language writing has become an important responsibility of school systems with growing immigrant populations. This book is full of stories told by teachers committed to this important work, showing what we've learned from our students and classroom practice. The stories come from teachers working with students who, as immigrants, have attended middle schools, high schools, and colleges in the United States. You will hear how we teachers guide our students to interact with text and with other writers, and how we respond to student writers and their writing. We're teaching composing, not literacy, at these levels of schooling, so the stories you'll encounter here will reflect that.

The "teachers' voices" telling these stories, including my own, are the spotlight of this book. The "frameworks" section in each chapter provides background information from the teaching profession, giving context to the voices. Think of these frameworks as the staging behind the action, sometimes painted in detail, other times done merely in large impressionistic brush strokes. "Investigations" also appear throughout to offer you ideas to ponder or tasks to try out when you put down the book.

This is an interactive text. The whole point is for you to hear about others' classroom experiences in order to generate new experiences and ultimately new knowledge on your part as a language teacher. So as you read this book, whenever you yearn for more information, go out and find it! If, as you're reading, you wish that you had been presented with more teacher voices, then go out and meet with a teaching colleague and talk about whatever is intriguing you. If, as you're reading, you wish that I had gone into more detail in a frameworks background section, then consult the list of suggested readings and find out more about the profession through your own research.

For more comprehensive views of the field of teaching writing to second- and foreign-language learners, see Ferris & Hedgcock (1998), Grabe & Kaplan (1996), Leki (1992), Reid (1993), and Scott (1996). For the down-to-earth voices of experience, read on!

1

REFLECTING ON YOUR OWN EXPERIENCE STUDYING WRITING

I wish I would be telling the truth if I said that nobody ever said writing would be easy. But I can hear Ms. Novak as clear as day: "All you have to do is follow your outline. It's easy." I even remember hearing her chipper voice in my dreams years later while I was struggling with my dissertation: "Just write one paragraph for each roman numeral from your outline. That's all you have to do." And it wasn't only Ms. Novak in English composition. Mrs. Black and Mr. Ferguson promised me that my outlines would guide me handily through essay writing in their social studies and Shakespeare classes. Even Madame Bernier—who was otherwise totally genuine in her acknowledgment that students learn languages in various ways, an uncommon notion in a school dedicated to audio-lingual language pedagogy—even she looked at me once when I came to her for help on a French essay and said, "Well, did you write an outline? That would make it easy."

That was the late sixties, and I figured there was a conspiracy in the teachers' room of my high school. Why else would all of them have been saying the same thing over and over? Along with all the other suspicions of that era, I just explained away Outlining Makes Writing Easy as a machination to keep anarchy out of our school and out of our impressionable minds. That was in my stronger moments. The rest of the time I assumed there was something wrong with me, that I couldn't write. Okay, I've got this outline, but how do I get one little phrase to turn into a whole paragraph? Once I force a paragraph out, the next point in my outline no longer seems to be the next logical step. So if I just give in and write my essay and then rewrite my outline afterward, will the teacher notice? I don't have any idea whatsoever how I came up with outlines to begin with. How do I know what I'm going to write before I try to write it? Why don't we ever talk about things that we might end up writing about? How am I supposed to come up with ideas for an outline out of thin air? There's no question it was high time for the pedagogical revolution to process.

If you're curious about the pendulum swing from product-oriented to process-oriented teaching within the field of teaching writing to native speakers of English, see Hairston's (1982) article, "The winds of change: Thomas Kuhn and the revolution in the teaching of writing."

But there were still a few years of product-oriented composition teaching to come. I remember being freed from outlining in college composition while studying with my laid-back progressive English professor, Mr. Armstead. Instead of diagramming sentences and repeating that the capital letters follow the roman numerals and the small letters follow the Arabic numerals, he sat on the edge of his desk at the front of the room and talked about the war, Kent State, and campesinos. We felt the rhythm of King's "I Have a Dream" speech and were moved by the power of language and its effect on individuals and society. Mr. Armstead got us to talk enough about the sociopolitical issues that we read about in our freshman anthology that I began having a sense that there were important things for me to write about and that I had interesting ideas about those things. But that feeling was fleeting. Every Friday Mr. Armstead gave us an essay topic, something that grew out of our week's readings and discussions, and told us it was due the following Friday. Not having a clue as to how to get going on a paper (except knowing that outlines didn't work well for me), I procrastinated the whole week, sweating about how I would get the paper done, feeling guilty that I wasn't doing anything about it. I'd inevitably crank out something Thursday night just in time for the Friday deadline. Meanwhile I remained very much involved in the course, inspired by the new readings and discussions that did not relate much—or so I thought—to what I was supposed to be writing about but that would serve as a basis for the next week's essay. I never turned in anything other than first drafts in college composition. Those first drafts were graded and returned the following Monday, and I never knew why I got the grades I did.

I finally learned ways to write academic papers in graduate school. Maybe I finally learned how to read and make connections among ideas from one source to another at that time since I was focusing on a unified course of study. A broad liberal arts education may have its merits, but I never read much of anything in depth as an undergraduate except German literature, given my major in that language. It was in graduate school that I began to see links between what I was studying in various courses, and I began to draw on my growing understanding of a field of knowledge to understand new readings and discussions. I also found that in reading and listening to discussions, I was able to learn new ideas as well as analyze how an argument was developed. I may well have developed the ability to analyze the structure of arguments during my undergraduate study of German literature. But what was new for me in graduate school was that I took my understanding of a framework of an argument and deposited that framework somewhere in my mind for later use as a rhetorical strategy for my own writing.

Besides analyzing the rhetorical structure of academic arguments and keeping that structure mentally shelved for later use in my writing, I attempted many other writing strategies throughout graduate school. I was always trying to make academic writing easier for myself, and the type of strategy I experimented with most often involved ways to get going on my writing early to avoid my undergraduate pattern of procrastination. I remember talking to professors early in a session about plans for term papers, then rushing home to try to capture the ideas on paper, sometimes simply in the form of random notes and sometimes as drafts of introductions for the actual paper. Next I'd gather more library information or perhaps some data, usually then letting the library sources and data sit on my desk and my ideas swim in my head for weeks. I'd end up throwing the paper together at close to the last minute. For each paper assigned I'd vow to work more steadily and efficiently the next time around.

The single strategy that I found most successful for managing the workload of writing was working in cooperation with fellow classmates. Setting a schedule with each other for regular meetings, bouncing ideas back and forth, trying things out in writing, collecting data, alternating trips to the library for more sources, writing and rewriting—it all worked out easier in collaboration with friends than when I suffered it on my own. Working with others I became far more aware of the process one needed to go through to produce good written work because we kept talking about the process in determining plans with each other from meeting to meeting. As I reflect on that period in my academic life I am pleased that I learned that I write best in collaboration with others, but I am disappointed that I was allowed very few opportunities to write collaboratively for required school assignments. Most of this work was done for conference presentations, publications, and curriculum development for teaching assistantships rather than for course term papers.

I've seen from examining my own history as a writing student that my early schooling, even into college, involved what we now refer to as product-oriented writing pedagogy. The focus of the teacher's and the students' attention was the final written product, the essay. There was little discussion or experimentation with various strategies for producing those final written products, except, of course, for the use of the outline, a static product in itself. As it turns out, I was most satisfied with my writing and I learned most when I ignored the constraining outline, despite what my teachers called for.

In my memories of high school English and freshman composition, I was not encouraged to draft and redraft, to evaluate my own writing, or even to determine my own reason or purpose for pitching a paper in a certain direction. I was only writing for the teacher, never to accomplish something in my own learning agenda. I wish my teachers had challenged me with more reasons to write, helping me determine what I wanted papers to accomplish. Rather than simplify things ("The only thing you have to do is. . .") I wish my teachers had pushed me to peek at the complexity of the range of directions and attitudes I could take in my writing, let alone the universe of ideas I could incorporate in my writing, and then I wish they had guided me in strategies for putting those attitudes and ideas into print. This is what takes place in the classroom given process-oriented writing pedagogy. The teacher works with students, sometimes individually, helping them try out alternatives, responding to them as autonomous writers, helping them experiment with various strategies to see what might work well given a variety of writing tasks, guiding them through multiple drafts until the students realize they have produced their best written work. Students also collaborate with each other, acting as resources, sounding boards, critics, and coauthors. Writing is not easy. The best writing teacher helps students realize many ways to confront the difficulties of writing, move past the difficulties, and understand what has been accomplished.

That's where I came from as a writer. My past shapes my present; my younger student-self informs my teaching-self. In upcoming chapters you will see more of my teaching-self, as well as those of my colleagues in middle school through university levels. My colleagues' and my own students, including those from my dissertation research, also appear in these pages. As part of any teacher's continuing professional development, it is important to critically reflect on one's own learning past in order to glean the best and adapt or diverge from the rest in controlled and justified ways. Think about it. What was your experience as a writing student?

It is important for all teachers to examine the sources of their pedagogical beliefs. We all approach our classrooms and students with ideas from our understanding of principles and methods of teaching, curriculum design, the structural and discourse patterns of English text, language learning and use, and other important areas in our professional field. We are also influenced in our teaching by our own classroom experiences as students. Take time now to collect memories of your experiences as a student in writing classes. In a later chapter you will be asked to reexamine the memories you document now in order to get a fuller view of your attitudes toward writing and teaching writing. Before reading further in this book, answer in as much detail as possible each of the following questions.

1 *What was your earliest classroom experience with learning how to write? How old were you? What were your school and class like? What were your fellow students and the teacher like? What do you remember most about what your teacher taught? What do you remember learning? How do you remember reacting to what happened during the classroom teaching and your learning?*

2 *What later significant school experiences with learning about writing or composition do you remember? Again, what do you remember most clearly about what your teacher taught you? How do you remember reacting to the instruction? What do you remember learning about writing or composing? What do you remember learning about yourself as a writer? Describe as many critical school experiences as you can.*

3 *How do you remember your teachers responding to your writing? How did they give you feedback? What did they say to you? What did they write on your papers? What areas of your writing did they focus on in their comments? How you remember feeling when you got their feedback? How did you respond to grades on your writing? How did teacher response and grades affect you as a writer in school?*

4 *As a student, which types of school writing assignments did you find easiest* to do? Which types of school writing assignments did you find most difficult? Why do you think these were easy or difficult? What is it about the types of writing assignments that might have made them easy or difficult for you? What is it about you as a writer that might have caused some assignments to be easy and others difficult?

5 How would you describe yourself generally as a student reader? Did you avoid reading assignments? Did you do some but not all assigned reading? Did you conscientiously accomplish all reading assignments? Did you do all assigned reading and even more on your own? How do you believe your reading habits as a student may have affected your writing?

6 How much writing do you remember doing alone as a student and how much in collaboration with fellow students? Do you remember which you preferred? Why?

7 Do you remember your writing in school ever being compiled in a "Best of. . ." volume or published in some way with other student writing? What were the circumstances? How did this experience affect you as a writer?

8 As an adult, what writing have you done that you really enjoy? Why do you enjoy it? What is it about the type of writing task or about you as a writer that made the experience pleasing to you? What strategies can you think of that you regularly draw on to do this enjoyable writing?

9 As an adult, what experiences have you had that pushed you to write something new? How do you go about tackling a new writing task? What strategies have you used to write something new? How did you feel about the task and yourself as a writer?

10 How would you describe your current adult self as a reader? What do you like reading most? What do you regularly read? How much time do you read weekly or daily? When you read various types of material, what do you focus on? (main points only? all of the ideas? only the interesting ideas? the author's use of language?) How do you think your current reading habits might affect you as a writer?

11 How much reading and writing do you do at a computer terminal? What are your experiences communicating by e-mail and getting information from the Internet? Do you notice yourself reading or writing differently or for different purposes, given the electronic technology, than when you read or write using paper?

Other Investigations

For a multimedia adventure, see Karen Johnson and Glenn Johnson's *Teachers Understanding Teaching* (1997), the multimedia hypertext CD-ROM component in the **TeacherSource** series. Johnson and Johnson's first five tasks suggest ways for you to reflect on your own learning background as a means of informing yourself as a teacher.

Suggested Readings

If you yearn for an optimistic view of U.S. public education, read Mike Rose's *Lives on the Boundary: The Struggles and Achievements of America's Underprepared* (1989). He begins with the story of his own life and schooling in the U.S. as the son of Italian immigrants and refocusses on the lives of all of our students.

For the voice of a Chinese teacher of English reflecting on her own educational background, see Danling Fu's *"My Trouble is my English": Asian Students and the American Dream* (1995). Besides her own story, Danling Fu tells the stories of three young refugees from Laos as they experience high school in the U.S.

2

ADDRESSING VARIOUS STUDENT WRITING PROCESSES

Any writing teacher, whether tutoring one-on-one or teaching a large class of students, needs to observe individual writers vigilantly in order to respond appropriately to their learning processes. The teacher's charge is to challenge each student writer in the best way at any given time. The first step is vigilance.

Let's take a close look at three student writers in particular. If you teach writing in the United States, any of these students could be either a current or past member of your class.

THREE ESL STUDENT WRITERS

Kim is a 23-year-old Korean student at a large California university. He's majoring in biology and taking a number of psychology classes as well. In the second term of his sophomore year, Kim has a grade-point average of 2.35. Kim's family immigrated to the United States from Korea twelve years ago. A native speaker of Korean, Kim attended three years of elementary school and both junior high and high school at English-speaking schools in California. He took ESL and mainstream content courses at these schools. He claims to speak a little Spanish, but has never taken a Spanish course in school.

Kim

I got to know Kim while I was doing my dissertation research. At that time, I learned from Kim what his prior experience studying English was like as he described for me activities he remembers from his former English classes. I was particularly interested in Kim's experience doing that very academic task of writing from sources: quoting, summarizing, paraphrasing, and everything else we do when writing from sources for college or other academic purposes. He distinguished between two ways of using background sources: reacting to the themes in the passages and using the information in the background passages to support his ideas. In psychology and philosophy courses Kim wrote papers summarizing background text (for example, pros and cons on an issue), concluding with his own opinions. He described papers for content courses like psychology and philosophy as being "easier and more fun" than those he has written in English class because the assignments included fewer requirements, allowing Kim more control and creativity in developing the papers. Kim complained that writing from background sources can be tedious if the background text is boring, and he claimed to favor writing from his own experience over writing from sources because the freedom to determine the content made writing easier.

I asked Kim about his experience doing academic writing in Korean. Kim said he had no experience writing from background sources in his first language. He studied in Korea only until the fourth grade and at ten years old came with his family to the United States. He reads and writes letters in Korean, but has never done any academic reading or writing in the language. Although Kim claimed not to know anything about academic language in Korean, he suspected that Korean writers use background sources differently because, he said, everything is different, even paraphrasing.

I had the opportunity to follow Kim closely as he wrote a paper in a content-based anthropology–ESL writing course. The "content-based" aspect of this ESL writing course means that the course materials that are read and written about all center around the field of anthropology. In other words, while developing their academic reading and writing abilities for the college level, Kim and his ESL classmates also learn about anthropology. After having read and discussed in class the first chapter of an undergraduate anthropology textbook by Marvin Harris (1995), Kim wrote a paper on the following topic:

TOPIC:

Imagine that you are an anthropologist preparing to observe and report on a subculture or societal group. Write a composition in which you explain which anthropological concepts you plan to consider in your report. Make your explanations clear enough for a university student unfamiliar with anthropology to understand. The subculture you are preparing to observe is that of fraternities and/or sororities at your university. Make reference to the Harris (1995) chapter as you explain the concepts that you choose.

Here is what I observed Kim doing as he wrote his paper: He quickly began writing his first paragraph after receiving the written topic, with very little planning. He followed a simple pattern for a five-paragraph essay relating three anthropological terms to fraternities, each term in its own paragraph in the body of the paper. First he put together a straightforward introductory paragraph that defined *subculture* and set up the topic as stated in the assignment. For each of the next two paragraphs, Kim searched the anthropology text for which term to discuss, paraphrased a definition for a first sentence of the paragraph, and completed the paragraph by relating the term to incidents in fraternity life. For the third term he asked me to explain part of the text, and then he completed his paragraph based on my explanation. Kim worked in a systematic and controlled manner, matching information from the text with his understanding of fraternities, and fitting that correspondence into a familiar five-paragraph composition structure. After meticulously creating and evaluating his prose phrase by phrase, Kim revised little. Kim seemed to have fair comprehension of the background text, but his confidence in his comprehension was lacking, as seen in his request for outside help in understanding. He did, however, exhibit a sense of control over his own simply structured written text.

Kim's paper can be read in Chapter 7, pp. 66-67.

June is a classmate of Kim's. June is a year older than Kim; at 24, she's a sophomore majoring in art, with a 3.30 grade-point average. June immigrated to the United States with her family six years ago, and she is a naturalized U.S. citizen. At home she speaks Mandarin, her first language, almost exclusively with her family, and she has no foreign or second language experience other than English. Before enrolling in the University of California, June attended a local community college for two years and a nearby state college for one year. She took ESL and breadth courses at these colleges.

June

I asked June the same questions I asked Kim, particularly about her experience writing from sources. June explained to me that she had never written papers using information from background texts. She went to college in Taiwan for one year, didn't write any papers, and is unaware how background sources are used in Chinese. June has never written a research paper in the United States, only book reports and papers critiquing art exhibits. She has never done any reading or library work for these papers, using only her notes from the art exhibits, including pictures that she drew as reminders. As Kim had done, June lamented the many rules and requirements for papers in English class versus other college courses, especially in her major. She feels more freedom writing papers in art classes than in English classes.

June's "freedom" in writing is relative, however. The way June puts it, she experiences constant psychological difficulties about writing in English. She worries about cultural misunderstandings, saying she is afraid her ideas will not be acceptable or will be misconstrued in this culture. She reported regular fears that people would laugh at her because of language errors in her writing except when she writes about the arts—she is confident that the strength of her ideas will outweigh the language difficulties.

June wrote the same paper Kim did about anthropology and fraternities and sororities. Like Kim, June had read the first chapter of the anthropology textbook by Harris (1995) and heard a discussion in class about the chapter before receiving the paper topic. But June had a big problem: she didn't understand much of the anthropology text at all. Even after getting the paper topic, June spent lots of time poring over the text, often examining sections that seemed of minimal relevance to the writing task. She did manipulate the background text to a certain extent by paraphrasing two brief sections. She also consulted the background text for spelling. However, she copied three sections of the background text without using quotation marks, including one section of two lengthy sentences. For two of the copied sections, June followed with a response to the copied passage using her own words, and in one case this response showed that June had misunderstood the anthropology text. Watching June write her paper

Take a look at June's paper in Chapter 7, pp. 68-69.

allowed me to see the struggle a person can go through when faced with a writing task based on background reading material that is way over his or her head.

Celia is younger than Kim and June by about eight years. She's a sophomore in high school, bilingual in spoken English and Spanish. At ten years old she immigrated to the United States with her mother and siblings from Venezuela. In a large urban elementary school, Celia was in ESL pullout courses for Spanish speakers for an hour or two every day and in mainstream classes the rest of the day. Once she began high school, Celia was no longer required to attend ESL classes. Now in her second year of high school, Celia tutors some of the high school students studying Spanish as a foreign language in exchange for their tutoring Celia in English grammar, an opportunity arranged by Celia's English instructor and the school Spanish instructor. At home Celia speaks Spanish with her mother and mostly English with her siblings. Once in a while she will go for a couple of days speaking only Spanish with her youngest sister, "so she remembers."

Celia

Celia's spoken English is sophisticated and sassy. She's into the gossip of rap and salsa from both Americas and can sit and chat on and on in English about world music. But writing is another story, as Celia admits. She remembers spending all weekend—Friday, Saturday, and Sunday—writing just the first draft of an essay for her English class about what an anthropologist wrote in an article about culture. Sometimes she writes first in Spanish and then translates into English; other times she uses phrases from her notes from class discussions, building sentences from the phrases. Whatever she does, doing a first draft of an essay, even a short essay, takes a long time. Celia complains about first drafts, but she loves getting help from her classmates on successive drafts of her papers and revising on the classroom computer. If it weren't for Celia's English writing workshop instructor's urging her to stop revising, turn in the essay, and move on to something else, she would happily keep revising any given assignment forever.

In Chapter 3, p. 29, you will see the assignment Celia refers to, based on an article by anthropologist Clyde Kluckhohn, suggested for use at the high school level by Hilles and Lynch (1997).

The stories of Kim, June, and Celia must remind you of student writers you've known in the past. What stories can you tell of other student writers and how they wrote?

The stories of Kim, June, and Celia are representative of other second-language writers in many ways, and in other ways, they are anomalous. In order to sort out common threads from anomalies we will consider some key concepts in the field of writing pedagogy, discussing these concepts in the context of language learners writing in English.

THERE IS NO SINGLE WRITING PROCESS
(OR WRITING IS LIKE PLAYING PINBALL)

One way to conceptualize writing processes generically is to think of a sequence of activities like the following:

planning
gathering information
drafting
revising
editing (or proofreading)

In fact, no one—native or nonnative speaker of any language—follows that sequence as the writing process. Depending on the writing task (for example, compiling a shopping list versus compiling an annotated bibliography, writing a letter versus writing an academic essay), the writer's experience carrying out those types of tasks, the pressure on the writer to produce a well-written product, and many other issues (time pressure, use of pen and paper or computer, language proficiency), the writer may vary drastically from that generic sequence and follow a very different writing process. For example, if I write a note to a friend about a party coming up at my house, I might do little or no planning—I might just dash off a quick greeting, one I've often written before, and I'd most likely list the vital details about when and where the party will take place. However, if I write a letter to a dean at my university about a controversial issue on campus, the planning I do changes dramatically. I will think about how I will begin the letter and approach the subject, I may talk to colleagues about their ideas, I will try out sentences and phrases. I may even put it off for a while until I'm feeling confident and strong. And not only does the amount and type of planning vary between writing a party invitation and writing a sensitive letter to a boss, all the other aspects of the generic writing process change as well.

Even given specific types of writing—for example, in the area of academic writing (versus business writing or fiction)—there is no single writing process that everyone follows. Instead of thinking about the writing process as if the one listed above or any other more generic writing process were the only one that existed, I prefer envisioning a pinball machine as a metaphor for writing processes.

Remember pinball—what we used to play in the old days before electronic video games? There's a knob you pull to make the metal ball spring into action, analogous to an assignment triggering the beginning of a student's academic writing process. The ball bounces here and there from one spot to the next, making lights flash and bells ring, which I like to imagine happens within a student writer's inquiring mind. The spots the academic-writing pinball bounces off include participating in class, reading course materials, doing library research, brainstorming, listing, clustering, drawing mind maps, talking to classmates, talking to the professor, searching the Internet, translating, doing more reading, studying lecture notes, starting a rough draft, daydreaming, getting help on a rough draft, drafting more, revising, revising, revising, printing, reformatting, spellchecking, editing, proofreading, and probably other activities I've neglected. Obviously I've listed these here in an order that helps you understand them as being part of a writing process. But the thing about the pinball machine is that the ball bounces off each point it touches in wildly varying ways. You never really know exactly what's going to happen next. You can plan for a certain sequence of events, but you might well find the whole process taking a very

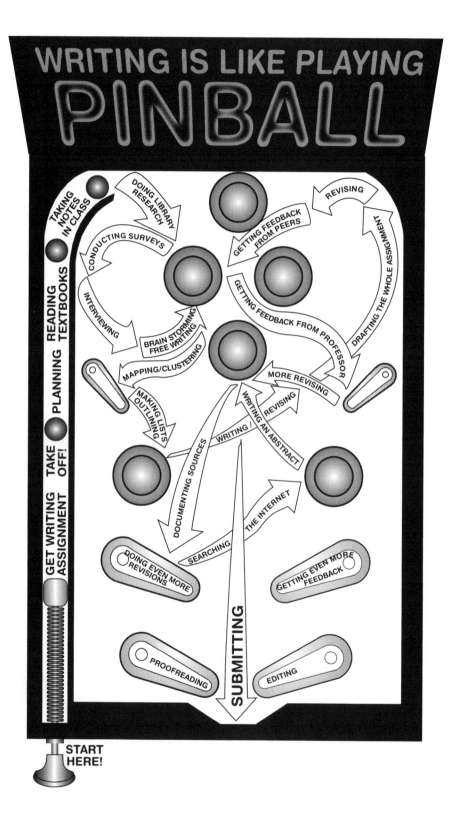

different course. Some students might think they can write a paper following the same process they went through for a different paper last semester, but it doesn't usually happen that way. So you just stick with it, pushing buttons, knobs, and flippers to keep the process going, sometimes bouncing off the same areas over and over and sometimes never hitting certain areas at all, sometimes accelerating, sometimes slowing down, until finally the pinball runs down the tube out of sight or you hand your paper to your professor. Whew!

Some might think writers can maintain more control over their own writing processes than players can maintain over a pinball game. After all, there are great writers out there—aren't they able to control the processes they go through when they write? No way. Even the greatest writing, the most natural, flowing, easily convincing, and intriguing prose that exists may grow out of wildly unpredictable and uncontrolled writing processes. Pick up a volume of *Writers at Work: The Paris Review Interviews*—you'll see what I mean. Pinball wizards figure out how to work through all the surprises of the game, responding appropriately to the process of the pinball game as it is taking place. So do writers.

BALANCING PROCESS AND PRODUCT PEDAGOGY

In the classroom, writing teachers need to do plenty of process work guiding the students through various strategies for working with text and writing well. Students need to experience lots of strategies for thinking about topic areas, getting started on rough ideas, sifting through ideas and beginning to organize them for writing, clustering, mapping, listing, outlining, drafting, rereading, redrafting, cutting and pasting, reworking, revisioning, revising on end, proofreading, editing. All of those aspects of a writing curriculum help students develop their writing processes. Then there are other activities that take place in writing classes: summarizing, paraphrasing, analyzing an author's approach or argument, retelling something from another perspective, and so on. For these components of the writing curriculum, the focus is on written products.

Kim would benefit from some analysis of academic essays demonstrating that there are other organizational structures for essays than the five paragraphs. June needs help trying out strategies for studying and learning from authentic academic text, like the anthropology text. Celia, at the high school level, could use help honing her revising process so she works more efficiently and comes to closure—finishing essays—more quickly and with more confidence. It is important to consider your particular teaching situation and your students' needs in order to determine the appropriate balance of process and product work in your writing classroom. In striking the balance between process and product pedagogy you will find that rather than teaching writing per se, or reading, or any other separate skill, what you are doing is guiding your students to interact with text.

L2 WRITING ISSUES

In addressing the needs of writers like Kim, June, and Celia, there are particular points to consider that may affect the students' writing processes because they are writing in a second language. Second-language writers tend to use a limited range of writing strategies, relying on previous successes rather than experimenting with alternative strategies in new writing situations. The extent to which they understand or misunderstand any background reading text or the writing assignment itself will surely affect the writing process—as will not just their understanding, but also their confidence in that understanding. Together, researchers refer to this understanding and confidence in that understanding as *authority*. In other words, second-language writers may lack authority over background reading text, not understanding fully, for example, as was the case for June. Or they may lack authority over their own emerging written text, unfamiliar with the genre or rhetorical approach, for example. It may, at times, be a matter of fitting into the second-language context, especially for writers from very different cultures, with different societal attitudes toward text, or with different experiences with background reading. In other cases, some second-language writers have little experience revising, instead proofreading all along from the first word of what others would call a "rough" draft. Yes, there are drawbacks that emerge in the writing processes of second-language writers. But the big advantage that our students have is the personal experience they bring to their writing to integrate as illustration, explanation, and insight.

What One Teacher Has Tried

> One thing I have learned through teaching writing is the way
> that context works. It's important for writing tasks, activities,
> and explanations, to be contextualized, but as importantly,
> the course development is also contextualized. Context, then
> works both internal to and beyond the walls of the classroom.

(KimMarie Cole, University of Wisconsin–Madison)

KimMarie Cole has gone to exceptional lengths to develop a writing course that meets the needs of individual students in her classes. "Class in a Box," as KimMarie calls it, is an innovative design for content-based writing courses at the college or adult levels, "individualizing instruction and creating space to work one-on-one with students." Instructors at middle and high schools are familar with this type of writing workshop environment from the work of Atwell (1987) and Calkins (1994). ESL instructors at colleges or adult schools are rarely assigned an exclusive classroom they can decorate and arrange workshop style. The need to carry course materials into and out of a classroom that also accommodates many other classes during the day is what drove KimMarie Cole to create her "Class in a Box."

Even before that, KimMarie's course emerged like a phoenix from a small student "revolt" in one of the writing classes she was teaching in a content-based language program. Her students' upset got KimMarie "thinking about content-based writing courses and the ways that the content interacted with the students' experience of the writing class." The details of the revolution in KimMarie's class are not crucial—if you haven't yet experienced a student revolt from the teacher's viewpoint, your time will come. KimMarie is to be commended for turning student action into an improved teaching and learning environment.

At the time of the student revolt, KimMarie had been teaching content-based writing courses in academic language programs for some time:

I tried a couple of different content areas for this course, areas that I thought would be interesting to the students and would be rich enough to generate writing and reading with easy access to outside sources (all important in my view to the development of effective academic writing). At the end of each semester, I conducted a supplemental evaluation (beyond that given by the school to evaluate the teacher's performance) to try and get at what the students thought of the various aspects of the class. Time and time again, a common concern was with the preselected, never-ending, single content focus. Students did understand the need to have something to write about, but most would not have chosen the content area that I did, and many got tired of it quickly. They didn't see how it fit with the rest of their academic work. One semester I tried a content area that was more closely related to their interests and academic goals (conflict management and resolution). That semester the complaints were that they already knew all this stuff and had classes about it. [Goldstein et al. (1997) found the same student complaints.]

In addition to content concerns, I had a growing awareness of different students' needs in terms of time and attention to aspects of the writing process. Some students had already developed very sophisticated personal heuristics for getting started, generating ideas, etc., but didn't know how to develop them. One Belgian student with a great fascination for computers set up complex mindmaps and very interesting visual displays of his topics but presented his paper in bullet form. Another Taiwanese woman was so frozen about getting started that she would make herself sick (literally) worrying about it and then rushed to do a paper that wasn't very good. Consistently, I had students who were reluctant to participate in class, or were culturally uncomfortable about participating, so it was never clear what they understood. A few students seemed to dominate discussions.

Another important consideration for me developed through a special course with intensive long-term conferencing with individual students working on term papers. I discovered that being a native speaker of English didn't really mean that I understood what a student "should" say or needed to write in terms of language correctness. Often when there were errors that have been called "global" in the literature, unpacking the student's ideas and finding out what they really wanted to say showed me over and over again that time was essential. Students whose language skills are developing need time to have someone listen to their ideas without presuming that a simple marginal note would or could suffice to clarify both writing (composing) and language issues that arose. I wanted more time in my large writing classes to spend with each student than even regular conferencing would allow.

I began to ask myself what was really important about the writing course: what I wanted students to be able to do; what I hoped they would come to understand, what kinds of skills and activities

I thought effective writers would need to do. Then I thought about ways that a whole course could constantly reinforce those kinds of practices, working in a spiralling fashion to aid in the development of critical reading and thinking; varied types of writing from the personal and anecdotal to the academic argument; researching skills—selection and evaluation of appropriate materials; and making choices. It seems that a lot of what a writer must do involves choosing. And I wanted to create a format that would allow students a certain autonomy and independence *and* allow me to spend more time with each of them.

As far as course preparation goes, "Class in a Box" involves a lot of teacher preparation up front. I wrote all of the mini-assigments, paper guidelines, and in-class essay questions. But well before that, I decided that it was quite important to have a "content" thread running through the course, so I selected readings from various readers, textbooks, and journals that could be used from various perspectives. For example, there were a couple of pieces on gun control that students could have used in a paper about gun control. One of those pieces, however, could have fit with different readings about health care in a paper about government responsibility. Another could have been combined with still other readings to be a source on the topic of personal freedom in different cultures. The idea of the readings was to have them stimulate thought and generate ideas—not for a single kind of paper, but to allow the students to, again, make choices. Concretely, for a semester-long class, there were 31 articles, each classified into one of five broad content areas (culture, education, language, power, and problems and solutions).

Additionally, the articles were all read and evaluated for which parts of the writing process they could illustrate. One article, for example, really did a good job of comparing and contrasting with lots of examples and development. Another had an excellent introduction that could serve as a model for organizing the structure of a paper. For each "mini-assignment" (the designation given to activities where the focus was on some aspect of writing development, some point), the students had to do four things: (1) read about the point (for example, "organization") from a couple of writing textbooks; (2) complete at least two activities using readings and apply their understanding of what they had read in the textbooks to some selected materials; (3) reflect in a journal on what they had learned and how they would use that new understanding; and (4) apply the concept in their own academic papers. The articles then contributed to step two of this process. Each task gave them the choice of several articles they could use as the source material. In practice, then, some of the students read different articles all the time. Others, noticing that some of the articles were cross-referenced for several activities, tended to use the same ones over and over, mining them for different purposes.

Compiling the "box" was another important activity before the class ever started. It meant organizing the articles, finding writing references and resources, and thinking ahead to a "library" system (checking out articles), developing a system for students to hand in their work and set up conferences during class time. The hand-in sheets helped the students and me with record keeping. It gave me an idea about what they wanted to conference about, what stage they were at in their writing, how they wanted the piece to be read. When I gave it back to them, it was either accepted or "not yet complete." That was the sign additional revisions were needed.

Since the course was individually paced, record keeping was critically important. I didn't realize at first how important it would end up being. Since I had previously taught courses that had uniform deadlines and assignments, the variety of things being turned in to me required a different kind of thinking. I look at journal writing, for example, differently than papers. When the folder of items to be read went home with me in the evening, I didn't know what I would find. Sometimes paper drafts, sometimes journals, sometimes mini-assignments. I noticed that semester that I needed to "reset" my reading often. In fact, that ended up being one of the challenges of the course for me. I think I realized it fairly early on in the semester, though, and was able to make the necessary adjustments. Initially, I just read what was in the folder, from top to bottom. Later I started sorting the pieces, grouping them into similar types of writing. I read the papers first, then mini-assignments, and journals last of all, since they all required different kinds of responses. In this class there was always something to read, but there was never an overwhelming quantity. That was one of the real benefits I experienced. The preparation was quite intensive before the class began, but once it was underway, there was minimal preparation, and the spacing and pacing of the reading made it possible to spend more time on each piece—and definitely it was possible to spend more time with each student.

This course was in a two-hour block. It was a busy class with lots of different things happening all over the room. The students had freedom to decide how to use their time and when to meet with me for my help. They soon realized when talking with me would be most expedient for their purposes. At the end of each class, there was a brief period of "closing down the box" where students returned books and articles (or checked them out), turned in papers, and did record keeping. The box was big and heavy. It was a cardboard box that photocopy paper had come in. It was filled with books and articles—straining at the edges. At first I had thought to put the box contents on reserve in the library, but it became clear that we had to have everything each class time. I took the responsibility of carrying it back and forth, but soon after the semester started, I noticed that there were always a few students around before class started. One or another would volunteer to carry the box. After class, someone always took it or my bag and we carried things back and forth. This is a very small event, almost too small to notice, but it seems to capture two things—a sense of community and a sense of ownership and responsibility for the materials.

I don't flatter myself that the students all became wonderful, enthusiastic writers. They were "doing school" in large part. What was different was that the course format had them "doing school" in ways that looked more like "doing writing" than it ever had before in my teaching experience. I don't know if they used the skills from writing class anywhere else in their lives, but I know that for four hours every week, they were practicing writing and acting as writers.

(KimMarie Cole)

 1 *Can you imagine teaching a content-based writing class with KimMarie Cole's "Class in a Box" scheme? What reading materials would you assemble in the box for a college freshman writing course for ESL students? What reading materials would you assemble for a secondary school integrated-skills ESL class with a reading-writing emphasis? What reading materials would you assemble for a middle-school integrated-skills ESL course?*

2 *Find an interesting English writing course at your school, talk to the instructor about getting permission to observe, and sit in on the class. Observe vigilantly, taking notes on particularly successful activities you might want to duplicate someday and your interpretation of student involvement in or response to the activities.*

Later, in a group, compare observations, finding out what insights each person gained from observing live classes, especially regarding student involvement in various writing activities.

3 *Make up a writing project (assignment) and a class activity:*

Imagine you are the teacher of your dream class and your dream students are working on a great writing project. Tomorrow you have class—now you need to plan an activity for your students that will further them along with their writing project.

Who are your students (age? language backgrounds? general proficiency level?) and what's the course (type of school? name/purpose of course)?

What's the writing project? What materials are your students using? How long will it take your students to do the project? When did you begin, and when will the project be completed?

What will you do for tomorrow's class activity that relates to the writing project, or somehow furthers the students along in the process of completing the project?

Considerations: principles of lesson planning; balancing process and product pedagogy; integrating reading and/or other skills; authenticity of materials, tasks, and writing project; making it fun and interesting; what else?

Suggested Readings

For inspiring rationale and design of writing workshop classrooms in middle schools and secondary schools, see Nancie Atwell's *In the Middle: Writing, Reading, and Learning with Adolescents* (1987); and Lucy McCormick Calkins' *The Art of Teaching Writing* (1994).

3

INTEGRATING WRITING AND READING THROUGH ACADEMIC WRITING

In Australia, the United Kingdom, and the United States, as well as in other countries where English is a medium of secondary- and college-level instruction, there is a significant ongoing call for second- and foreign-language teachers to teach academic writing. Sometimes the call is uninformed and blind ("Students can't write a grammatical sentence in English!") and sometimes it is forward-looking ("Our first-year students need guidance in reporting on research done across the disciplines at our college, which they will be required to do in upper-division courses."). Teaching academic writing involves working within the school system and carrying out a range of responsibilities, from meeting (and sometimes establishing) curricular standards to helping students use facilities such as computer labs and libraries. It also involves responding to never-ending stacks of papers (more on that in chapter 7). Whether in a secondary school, a private language institute with college-bound students, or a college or university, the academic writing teacher's tasks center around challenging students to interact with written text (composing, reading, summarizing, paraphrasing, synthesizing, alluding to, reporting on, and so forth) in sophisticated, knowledge-generating ways.

Melinda Erickson integrates reading into her writing courses for freshman writers at the University of California at Berkeley for many reasons, not the least of which is that the writing pedagogy of UC–Berkeley College Writing Programs calls for it. Beyond that, Melinda has her own rationale for getting students to interact with written text and makes sense of her own teaching practice of integrating reading into her freshman writing courses in the following ways.

Overriding Melinda's rationale is the notion of student need, that reading is a primary demand of the university on students' time and study energy. That demand continues throughout all students' college careers and cannot be ignored. Moreover, readings Melinda brings into her courses function in a number of pedagogically useful ways. For example, readings provide authentic examples of text demonstrating issues that Melinda's entire class examines together, such as usage of vocabulary, sentence structure, rhetorical modes (comparison, contrast, persuasion), other discourse units (essay introductions, conclusions, literature reviews), the writer's audience, and purpose. When Melinda has her students examine these types of issues in readings, they are analyzing the readings as model written products, practicing the types of analyses the students need to also consider regarding their own writing.

Melinda also uses readings as springboards for discussion, having the students come up with their own personal viewpoints on themes reflected in the readings. Melinda's teaching beliefs are grounded in her training in teaching English for Academic Purposes (EAP), where the academic situation in which language is being used and student need are paramount in curriculum development. Yet these activities integrating reading and writing that Melinda does in her freshman composition course are reminiscent of my freshman composition course two decades ago (Chapter 1, p. 2), which was taught by a graduate student in British and American literature who developed curriculum based on how text can inspire social change.

But Melinda integrates reading and writing in other ways that I did not experience. She selects readings that will work well, analyzing language use with the whole class, readings that satisfy other criteria as well. She chooses readings representing a variety of written genres—for example, essays, journal articles, newspaper articles, letters, book reviews. It is this range of genres in selected readings that illustrates for student readers the variety in writers' audiences and purposes.

Melinda also selects readings according to the themes presented. Readings about related themes offer Melinda's students the opportunity to synthesize information from a variety of sources. Also, when the students integrate background resources into their own writing, Melinda helps them practice conventions of academic citation.

Teaching on a writing faculty including applied linguists like herself, as well as scholars in English literature and education, language, and literacy, forces Melinda to compare her pedagogical beliefs to those of fellow freshman composition teachers from other disciplines. Melinda has considered how she uses fiction as reading material in her freshman writing courses for English language students versus ways fiction might be used in English literature classes. Melinda's writing assignments differ from literary analysis, where students look at issues such as character development and stylistic influences on the author. Instead, Melinda engages her students with the ideas of the text and then uses the text later for analysis of audience, purpose, rhetorical structure, and other elements of academic written products.

Very early in the term, for example, Melinda and her students might be reading Bharati Mukherjee's *Jasmine* (1989), discussing choices the characters in the book have made, what motivated them, and what resulted from their choices. (*Jasmine* is a novel about a young Hindu woman who moves to New York and later to Iowa, and transforms into a new person in a new culture.) The related assignment might be for the students to write about a significant choice they have made. Another task for Melinda's students might be to survey Mukherjee's other works of fiction, either in the library resources or in the campus bookstores, since Mukherjee teaches at Berkeley.

Instead of doing literary analysis, Melinda's students work with text she has selected based on how relevant the themes might be to them, given their general age and life experience. She includes fiction and nonfiction by writers from the San Francisco Bay area, writers her students might meet, attend a reading or lecture by, or see on campus. She collects or has the students collect related readings, such as reviews of a book or interviews with the author, or writings by former students who also studied the book. Melinda invites the author to visit campus and speak to her students. As she says, "I'd like to shorten the distance between the students and the readings."

Heeding Melinda's advice and her students' glowing praise, I used Ben Fong-Torres's (1994) *Rice Room* as a springboard for discussion and writing one recent semester in a freshman composition course. *The Rice Room: Growing up Chinese-American: From Number Two Son to Rock 'n' Roll* is San Francisco journalist Ben Fong-Torres's autobiography of his first forty-some years. Everybody loved it. No matter where he or she was from, each one of my students identified in some way with Fong-Torres and his life growing up with his Chinese parents in Oakland. Over about three weeks I watched my students read for the authentic purposes of scanning for specific information, getting the gist, doing research, and enjoying a book. They wrote and rewrote, revised and edited, wrote under time pressure in class, and rewrote all over again, refocusing on the reading material from a different perspective.

It was easy for us to jump into the book. I brought in an old copy of *Rolling Stone* magazine and showed my students the cover article by Fong-Torres, and they immediately wanted to read about him. After we got through the first few chapters, in which we meet Fong-Torres as Ben, a small boy in Oakland's Chinatown, we spent a class session anticipating what issues would emerge from the rest of the book. (Or, better, what we hoped we'd find out more about.) We ended that class session with the students freewriting about an interesting aspect of our class discussion:

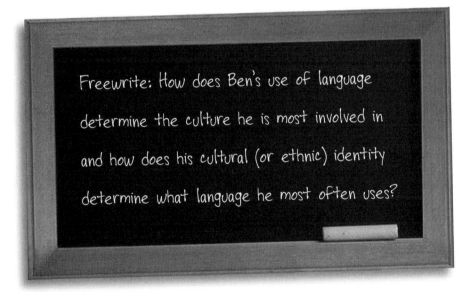

Freewrite: How does Ben's use of language determine the culture he is most involved in and how does his cultural (or ethnic) identity determine what language he most often uses?

For the following class session I had formalized an out-of-class essay assignment, a topic that had grown out of the students' expressed interests in the book. Here's what that assignment looked like, along with a corresponding revision guide, and other related writing topics that emerged from our class discussions over a period of about three weeks. By examining the student handouts you can see how the class explored the ideas in the autobiography from a number of vantage points.

ESSAY TOPIC:

Re: Ben Fong-Torres's <u>Rice Room</u>
In characterizing Ben's experience changing cultures, discuss the extent to which Ben grows up using the Chinese language, within the Chinese culture. Also characterize Ben's cultural situation other than Chinese (is it purely "American," or some multicultural mix, or what?).

GETTING STARTED: Skim the first 181 pages of <u>Rice Room</u>, taking notes about Ben's use of English vs. Chinese. Reread your freewriting from 9/24. Highlight relevant ideas. Reread your previous journal entries about <u>Rice Room</u>, highlighting relevant ideas. Think about how these ideas about language and culture overlap.

DUE DATES:

10/1	See "Getting Started" above. Bring notes from doing all of that to class. We'll brainstorm ideas about how you might approach the topic.
10/3	Bring two copies of your rough draft for peer review to be done in class.
10/8	Revise your paper according to your classmates' comments, and bring a newly revised copy for Cherry.
10/9–10/10	Individual conferences with Cherry on your writing.
10/10–10/14	Revise over & over; make an appointment to see Cherry for help.
10/15	Bring newly revised draft to class for proofreading.
10/17	Final draft due for a grade.

EVALUATION CRITERIA:

- How completely and complexly you've addressed the topic;
- How you've set the scene/issue/context at the beginning of your writing;
- How you've developed your paragraphs;
- How one paragraph leads to the next;

- How an overall thesis <u>unifies</u> your writing and how <u>distinctive</u> that thesis is;
- How you've presented the significance of your ideas in your conclusion;
- Distinction between your ideas and those of Ben Fong-Torres or any other author;
- How appropriate the grammar, word choice, spelling, and punctuation are;
- How the title reflects your particular thesis (again, a mark of distinction).

NOTE:

It is necessary that you distinguish any other author's ideas or words from yours using phrases like "according to . . ." or "So-and-so says . . ." However, footnotes and bibliography are not necessary for this assignment.

Also, remember to check pp. 309-311 in your handbook for how to prepare your typed essay.

After a few days of thinking, planning, and drafting, along with a class session devoted to brainstorming, students brought rough drafts to class for revision work in pairs:

REVISION GUIDE FOR BEN FONG-TORRES ESSAY: 10/3

You know the procedure: Read once quickly; read again slowly taking notes about each point on this guide; talk to each other giving your advice; take notes so you can use the advice you get in revising at home.

1. Has your classmate characterized Ben's experience changing cultures in a broad, expansive way? Has he/she written about the complexities of Ben's life (rather than simplifying Ben's life down to a few points)? Has your classmate discussed both Ben's language use and his cultural situation in a full and complete way? <u>Suggest ways your classmate might improve in these areas.</u>

See Chapter 6, pp. 51-56, for a view of students using this type of revision guide.

2. How well has your classmate set the scene at the beginning of his/her essay? In other words, how well has he/she provided context for us as readers to understand the main thrust of the paper? <u>Make suggestions about how the beginning can be improved— imagine you have never read Ben's book, and make suggestions from that standpoint.</u>

3. What do you think about the paragraphs in the essay? Are they long and completely developed? Are claims clearly stated and well-supported with evidence? Can you find topic sentences in the paragraphs in the body of the essay? <u>Suggest ways your classmate can improve the paragraph development in this essay.</u>

4. Are the paragraphs in the essay logically ordered? Does one paragraph lead clearly to the next paragraph? <u>Suggest places where your classmate might include transitions or other devices to connect the paragraphs more clearly.</u>

5. Does the conclusion do more than simply summarize what's already been said? Does it discuss the significance of the essay? Does it discuss implications from the major claims in the essay? <u>Suggest ways your classmate can make his/her conclusion more substantial.</u>

6. *****IMPORTANT***** How's the thesis? Does it do more than simply restate the assigned topic? Does it unify the whole paper? Is it distinctive? <u>Talk about how to get the thesis to the point where it accomplishes all of the above things.</u>

7. Are there any places in the paper where you are not certain whether the idea came from your classmate or from Ben Fong-Torres or from some other writer? <u>Suggest places where your classmate needs to clarify the distinction between his/her ideas and those of other authors.</u>

8. Is there a title yet? How well does the title reflect the thesis of this particular paper? How distinctive is the title? <u>Suggest ways to specify the title so it more directly relates to the thesis of this particular person's essay. If there is not a title yet, help your classmate compose a good, distinctive title.</u>

After several more days of revising and an individual conference with me on the in-progress draft, students brought close-to-final drafts to class for proofreading:

GUIDE TO PROOFREADING YOUR PARTNER'S PAPER: 10/15

1. Have your partner explain whether there is any aspect of this paper that he or she is still working on other than simple proofreading (more interesting introduction? more unifying thesis? more explanation in the paragraphs in the body of the paper?). Discuss these things, <u>giving your partner suggestions</u> about what he/she might do to improve things.

2. Read through your partner's paper, underlining problems you see with spelling, grammar, word choice, punctuation, etc. If you're not certain whether there's a mistake, write a question mark next to the place you're thinking about.

3. Trade papers with your partner so that you can look at your own paper, taking note of the places on your paper that your partner underlined (or where he/she jotted down a question mark). If you don't understand what your mistake is, ask your partner. If he/she is not able to explain the mistake completely, ask Cherry. <u>Reminder:</u> Use your own personal proofreading checklist at home to do more proofreading on your own paper. Proofread for one error at a time.

On the same day, students practiced writing under time pressure:

TIMED WRITING   10/15

Answer the following three questions about <u>Rice Room</u>. One long paragraph for each question is enough. Refer to examples in <u>Rice Room</u> to explain your answers.

1. Explain the significance of the rice room and "number two son," both of which are from the title of the book.

2. Explain what Ben's relationship with his parents is like by the end of the book.

3. How does Ben's experience growing up relate to yours?

Later in the term, some students chose to rework their essays for more complex writing purposes:

FOLLOW-UP ESSAY TOPICS

1. To expand your essay about Ben Fong-Torres, interview someone from your ethnic heritage about his or her use of language and their cultural identity here in the United States. Compare and contrast that experience with what you wrote about Ben Fong-Torres in your earlier essay. (Determine your interview questions according to issues you wrote about in that earlier essay so that you gather detailed interview information that you can relate to what you already wrote.)

2. Using library sources, find some of the articles Ben Fong-Torres was working on during the period of his life that he reported on in Rice Room (e.g., the award-winning Ray Charles piece and, if possible, pieces from East West). In your paper, analyze the articles you select in light of the life experiences Ben was going through at the time he was writing the articles.

For preparing ESL high school students for this type of college-level thinking and writing, Hilles and Lynch (1997) suggest an intriguing set of activities involving students in the analysis of culture. Beginning with visuals from *National Geographic*, the class does brainstorming and clustering tasks around what culture is and what it does (or how it functions). After generating and prioritizing definitions and functions of culture in small and whole-class groups, the student groups compare their lists with the whole class. Hilles and Lynch describe the ensuing class discussion, which

> explores which characteristics are important or superficial. The final step in this stage is to lead the class to a consensus regarding the benefits of understanding another culture and what potential problems might exist between cultures. Teachers should encourage students to explore how culture can be used to define an individual and if there are any dangers in allowing a culture to speak for an individual. (Hilles and Lynch, 1997, p. 375)

Following this stage of getting into the topic area of culture, the high school students are assigned reading passages jigsaw style, such that each group of students is responsible for studying and reporting on a particular section of the passage as a whole. Hilles and Lynch suggest, as an example passage, an excerpt from Kluckhohn's (1949) "Mirror for Man," in which Kluckhohn explains the anthropologist's perspective on culture and culture's effects on people in various societies. Among other possible procedures, Hilles and Lynch propose that jigsaw "group members become experts on their portion of the text. The groups are then reconfigured, with one expert in each group. In the reconfigured groups students construct a complete definition of culture, drawing on the specialized knowledge of each of the experts in their group" (1997, p. 375).

Once students have worked through the Kluckhohn text sufficiently, Hilles and Lynch suggest an activity to take the high school students beyond the text, to apply its ideas in other contexts:

> Students can assume the role of a stranger—or even of an alien. In this role they observe and record the everyday academic and social behaviors of their multicultural peers (including native English-speakers) and the reactions of others. They keep journals, produce a group report or paper, or put on a television show in which their subjects are interviewed or observed in their natural settings. (Hilles and Lynch, 1997, p. 375)

For Celia's response to this assignment, see p. 10 and p. 69.

As we saw with the activities used by both Melinda Erickson and myself with college students, the students involved in Hilles and Lynch's high school activities will interact purposefully and communicatively with each other and with background text as their written ideas emerge.

Consider ways that Hilles and Lynch's activities for high school ESL writers prepare those writers for college-level writing activities like those focusing on Mukherjee's Jasmine *(1989) (p. 22) or Fong-Torres's* Rice Room *(1994) (p. 23-28).*

For many language teachers, teaching academic writing resembles how they teach writing in other course contexts, for example, in creative writing or integrated multiskills language courses. Similarities may include a process approach assuming lots of student writing and rewriting, individualization of instruction to address a variety of student needs, and other issues already discussed in this book. In this chapter we'll take a look at frameworks for teaching academic writing that distinguish themselves from those for teaching writing in other contexts.

DEVELOPING ASSIGNMENTS

The major writing assignments a teacher of academic writing develops are crucial because they end up serving as curricular units. In other teaching contexts a writing assignment might simply be a topic ("Write an essay/poem/memo about XYZ") that provides a complex integrated final task culminating a language unit or curricular segment. But in academic writing courses, the well-planned writing assignment goes beyond the topic to include ideas for in-class time devoted to getting started, doing research, revising, proofreading, and other aspects of students' writing processes. A major assignment in one of my courses may take weeks to complete with all the activities it generates. Expectations as to what the final product needs to cover are also important to clarify because of the evaluative requirements of school obliging its writing teachers to grade their students. Not all academic writing teachers spell out such information on their assignment sheets the way I do; even if they remain implicit or are uncovered or negotiated later in the term, major writing assignments do entail practicing strategies for getting through the production of the product and being graded on the work.

It's unlikely that a writing topic such as "How I spent my summer vacation" would ever be assigned in a course in history, science, or even psychology. College or high school students studying those disciplines end up writing in-class exams and term papers about the concepts in those fields, responding to topics that history, science, or psychology professors think will make the students reflect on each field (or at least the sphere of the course), organize what they're learning, and usually apply what they're learning in some way. At the college and secondary levels the academic writing teacher needs to develop assignments that get students to write about issues in academic disciplines, demonstrating the knowledge they've gained from the course, and supporting their ideas with both personal experience and information from other writers or lecturers. The point of academic writing courses is to nudge the writer away from only thinking and writing about personal experience toward using text (Leki & Carson, 1997).

The best academic writing assignments are content-based and authentic. Such assignments require the students to work with content (in written form or from lectures, video, CD-ROM, or the Internet) in ways that reflect what the rest of the educational system expects. To look at it another way, content-based authentic writing assignments require the college or college-bound student to do reading and writing of the sort that they will be expected to do for instructors and professors across the curriculum.

To determine authenticity of assignments it is necessary to find out what the instructors or professors teaching breadth requirements are assigning their students. Surveys of academic writing assignments across universities can help here (Bridgeman and Carlson, 1984; Hale et al., 1996; Leki and Carson, 1997). But more important, I believe, is for academic writing instructors to consult with their colleagues across campus (or across town for those teaching college-bound students outside a college campus setting). Find out what the actual assignments are in general education courses in various disciplines, and update your information each year. For college or high school campuses with flourishing writing-across-the-curriculum programs, this is easily done. On other campuses—on most campuses, I'm afraid—it can be extremely difficult. Collaboration can give way to surveillance too easily in many academics' minds.

It's possible that many academic writing teachers will feel that authentic writing assignments would overwhelm their students. I agree that sequencing tasks is fundamental in any given curriculum. If authentic assignments are too complex for your students, then make their assignments realistic at least. The writing assignment from Chapter 2 on anthropology and fraternities/sororities (p. 8) was not an authentic assignment; that is, I do not believe an anthropology professor would ask students to write about such a topic in an anthropology course. But I think the use of content, the application of unfamiliar to familiar ideas, and the exposition required of the writers make it a realistic assignment, one that is similar to assignments that are actually assigned in other disciplines. And the example assignment embedded in my course materials from earlier in this chapter about Fong-Torres and the Chinese language and culture? It's possible that the topic from that assignment might be considered authentic for an ethnic studies course. Take another look at the core topic:

> In characterizing Ben Fong-Torres's experience changing cultures, discuss the extent to which he grows up using the Chinese language, within the Chinese culture. Also characterize Fong-Torres's cultural situation other than Chinese (is it purely "American," or some multicultural mix, or what?).

There's some ambiguity and leeway that I worked hard to build into that topic because I see plenty of that type of fuzziness in authentic writing topics from all disciplines. Part of what we as a class worked on with that assignment was interpreting the topic's ambiguity and leeway so students could start to understand how to judge the expectations of other writing topics from other professors. I admit that whether the topic in its entirety is truly authentic might be questionable. But the fuzziness of the topic, it seems to me, is an important aspect of authentic academic assignments.

Think of specific writing assignments you have given or you know other teachers have given. What level of student and type of course was it? To what extent were the assignments content-based and authentic (or realistic)?

HEURISTICS AND BACKGROUND SOURCES

There is no question that content-based authentic writing assignments can cause students to panic. As the teacher you need to pull out all the educational psychology you know and work on ways to help students calm down when they are given what they see as a difficult assignment. Only then can you begin getting the students to interpret the core writing task and whatever other work goes along with preparing to write, all the so-called *heuristics*, or ways of getting started.

Heuristic is a great word because of its sense of *finding out about* or *discovering* things. Getting students going is often the biggest challenge facing the process-oriented teacher. Likewise, getting going on a paper is often the biggest challenge facing the college student. Thankfully, we're far enough along with process writing as a pedagogy that there are plenty of student textbooks with lots of ideas for the huge range of activities that take place before something's written down and officially called The Paper. Prewriting, generating ideas, listing, clustering, cubing, planning, mapping, freewriting, journaling, journeying, whatever you want to call it, it's usually called "brainstorming" by our students. I like *heuristic* better than *brainstorming* because I've never been able to conjure up a sufficiently loud atmosphere in my classroom to call what's happening a collective brainstorm. In my classroom there's quiet talk, speculation, murmuring, mumbling, and an occasional excited remark of revelation. Discovery, yes; storming, no.

Drawing students into an area of thought and written discussion through readings makes pedagogical sense in the academic writing classroom. Get students to grapple with text studying background readings and they'll have ideas to grapple with in their own emerging written text. In the last chapter we saw Kim and June demonstrating varying degrees of authority (understanding and confidence in that understanding) over the text of their writing assignment. June had little understanding and little control over the content of the anthropology text. She also struggled with her own writing to such an extent that we can assume she had little authority over her own text. Kim, on the other hand, showed some understanding of the anthropology text, but he didn't quite trust that understanding—again, a mark of a lack of authority. Kim did, however, show authority over his own writing of his own text—he used a simple five-paragraph essay formula to demonstrate some simple understanding of the anthropology text. Both students needed to develop a sense of authority over the anthropology text in a heuristic stage of writing. With the strength of that authority, the students are better prepared to manipulate the ideas and text from the anthropology chapter in producing their own writing.

GETTING STUDENTS TO ADDRESS TOPIC AND AUDIENCE WHILE DEVELOPING THEIR OWN PURPOSE

For our students' academic writing to be strong, the students need to be writing something meaningful. They need to be saying something that demonstrates their understanding of the information they're learning about, and they need to show that what they're saying is important. That's what writing teachers mean when they talk about *purpose*: something important that's being said in the paper. Purpose is a reason why the student is writing the paper—besides the fact that it's an assignment. For many writing teachers purpose ends up being the most fundamental issue for students to work on in drafting and revising. We'll be looking at purpose in more detail in Chapter 7.

For ESL writing students in college and in college-bound secondary school classes, one goal of academic writing courses is often to write a term paper, sometimes on a topic of the student's own choosing. I am firmly in favor of building a term paper project into the academic writing curriculum, but I question open student-choice topics. Once again, the issue is how authentic the assignment is. From my observations I see undergraduates responsible for responding to professors' assignments more often than developing their own paper topics (as graduate students often do). There is certainly no shortage of advice in college rhetorics on narrowing paper topics. But interpreting assigned topics (versus choosing one's own topic) and interpreting the underlying expectations of the professor doing the assigning of the topic and audience are more important issues for us to work on in academic writing courses. The goal is for our students to develop an awareness during the writing process of ways to interpret topics from professors; to write on those topics in complete and accurate ways; and to formulate the writing, taking into account the knowledge and role of the professor/audience.

1 *In Chapter 7 we'll meet Amy Tickle from Michigan State University. Meanwhile, take a look at one of her writing assignments for ESL students in a content-based academic writing course focusing on the environment:*

> Topic: Write your congressperson, persuading him or her about an environmental issue.

Think about the audience for this paper: What kinds of things will Amy's students need to do in their writing to address the audience given for that assignment? And what about the writing purpose—do you expect Amy's students to be able to develop their own purposes for their writing? How do you think this assignment might be adapted for a secondary-school college-bound academic writing course?

2 *Compare my set of assignments on Fong-Torres's* Rice Room *(pp. 23-28) with the activities presented by Hilles and Lynch on culture (pp. 28-29). To what extent is each content-based and authentic? Compare ways the students are encouraged to get started (heuristics); the types of background readings; and issues of topic, audience, and purpose.*

3 *With a group of classmates or teaching colleagues, make up an academic task for students that integrates reading and writing.*

First, determine in your group (1) a general course type (evening adult school, secondary-level college preparatory, middle-school pull-out ESL, intensive private school for adults, college writing, or your choice) and (2) the general level of student (beginning, intermediate, advanced).

Next, develop an assignment that would be appropriate for the student group you've chosen, and write it out as you might for your students. Be sure it's clear how reading is integrated into the project. While you're at it, discuss and take note of classroom activities you could carry out before and after distributing the actual written assignment, making this a unit or module around your writing assignment.

Note: If you choose to develop your writing assignment for students in secondary- or college-writing courses, as you work out your reading material, consider how you can use authentic academic writing (academic textbook or journal material). Many teachers use newspaper material as background text for academic writing tasks. I've often had success using editorials, which are unified, well-developed prose; however, most other sections of the newspaper, especially news stories, are not developed following rhetorical patterns of academic text. This experience leads me to use editorials from newspapers to supplement academic textbook and journal discourse, if I use them at all. Think about what you, as the teacher, will do about selecting reading material for background sources.

4 *Now analyze the assignment you're developing from investigation #3. Think about each of the following sets of questions, and revise your assignment as you see fit. Keep your student population and course goals in mind.*

    a. Look at how you and your group composed the written assignment to hand out to students. How clear is your wording? What ambiguities remain in your wording of the assignment? Anticipate anything your students will not understand in what you've written. Also anticipate questions your students will have. Count on "how long does it have to be?" and figure out how you will address that popular query.

    b. Analyze the topic of your assignment. What is the core of the topic? (What's the main thing the students will need to write about?)

    c. What else will the students write about besides the core issue(s)? (What other ideas or issues will the students write about that might end up being peripheral but still necessary to the core topic?)

    d. Why will the students write this assignment? Think of a reason or purpose for your students to write, besides that it's a requirement for school. What are some ideas that would be worthwhile for the students to write about? Brainstorm any bright ideas you can come up with as a test to see how accessible your topic may be to your students. If you can't think of anything to write, can you really expect your students to find something to say?

    e. Who will the students write to (or for)? In other words, who's the audience? Do you want to make this intended audience explicit in your written assignment to your students? Why or why not?

    f. What types of heuristics (activities for getting started) would you encourage a whole class to try for this assignment? reading strategies? listing? mapping? diagrams? charts? journal entries? library research? Did you include ideas for heuristics in your actual written assignment? Why or why not?

    g. If you were working individually with a student who is having trouble getting going with this paper, a student who usually follows a step-by-step linear writing process, how do you think you would encourage that student to get started on the assignment?

    h. What could you, as the teacher, plan as a class activity to help further this writing task? Think of an activity to help students begin what some call an inner dialogue and others call dialogical thinking—the open, pro-con, or question-answer-new-question thinking that can lead to elaborate and well-developed writing.

i. Any ideas about how these student papers might ultimately be evaluated? By you as the teacher? By the individual writer? By the rest of the students in class? By someone else? Given the student group you've chosen, is it appropriate to consider grading the student papers at all? What criteria might you use to evaluate the final products? Do you think it is appropriate to include an indication of those evaluation criteria in the original assignment that you distribute to the students? Why or why not?

j. To what extent would you want students to anticipate a specific product before writing? To what extent would you want them to discover along the way what the final written product can become?

Suggested Readings

For more on teaching academic writing, see Grabe and Kaplan's *Theory and Practice of Writing* (1996). Teachers of middle school in particular will be interested in Chapter 10, and teachers in secondary school and college settings, Chapters 11 and 12.

For generating ideas for curriculum development of academic ESL writing courses, there are a number of helpful articles: Brinton, Goodwin, and Ranks (1994); Roen (1989); and Shih (1986). Also helpful for curriculum development in lower levels is Early, Thew, and Wakefield's *Integrating Language and Content Instruction K–12: An ESL Resource Book* (1986), and for college-level ESL instructors investigating the discourse of the university, Swale's *Genre Analysis: English in Academic and Research Settings* (1990).

4

INTEGRATING WRITING AND READING THROUGH CREATIVE WRITING

For my birthday, Penny gives me a diary, complete with a little lock and key to keep what I write from the eyes of all intruders. It is that little lock—the visible symbol of the privacy in which the diary is meant to exist—that creates my dilemma. If I am indeed to write something entirely for myself, in what language do I write? Several times, I open the diary and close it again. I can't decide. Writing in Polish at this point would be a little like resorting to Latin or ancient Greek—an eccentric thing to do in a diary, in which you're supposed to set down your most immediate experiences and unpremeditated thoughts in the most unmediated language. Polish is becoming a dead language, the language of the untranslatable past. But writing for nobody's eyes in English? That's like doing a school exercise, or performing in front of yourself, a slightly perverse act of self-voyeurism.

    Because I have to choose something, I finally choose English. If I'm to write about the present, I have to write in the language of the present, even if it's not the language of the self. As a result the diary becomes surely one of the more impersonal exercises of that sort produced by an adolescent girl. These are no sentimental effusions of rejected love, eruptions of familial anger, or consoling broodings about death. English is not the language of such emotions. Instead, I set down my reflections on the ugliness of wrestling; on the elegance of Mozart, and on how Dostoyevsky puts me in mind of El Greco. I write down Thoughts. I Write.
(Hoffman, 1989, pp. 120–121)

One of life's greatest releases is to express oneself in writing. Self-expression is therapeutic for everybody, and putting what needs to be said down in print gives that release a stamp of emphatic approval. And what is it like writing for creative release in a second or foreign language? "Freedom!" a student of mine once told me. On the other hand, consider Eva Hoffman, an adolescent having immigrated with her family to the west coast of Canada, choosing to write her personal journal in English rather than her native Polish for pragmatic reasons. In her second language, the adolescent Hoffman's journal becomes impersonal, even though it seems to her most appropriate written in her new language. And other students?

I've had students write poems and descriptive narratives of their past lives. I've often found that, unlike young native English speakers, my ESL students are not lacking for an experiential base from which to create stories. Perhaps this is the best reason for focusing on descriptive writing: our ESL students have so much to tell that it clearly is a strength! (Ron Balsamo)

Ron Balsamo teaches ESL and English courses at Santa Rosa Junior College in northern California. Like Melinda Erickson at Berkeley (Chapter 3), Ron teaches with colleagues who have English literature backgrounds.

If a student can creatively turn a phrase, that will go a long way toward forgiving the more "pedantic" grammatical or structural aspects of writing in the eyes of the English professor. I've all too often witnessed English professors overlooking writing problems in their native-speaking students that always seem to drive them wild in the writing of their nonnative-speaking students. Why? Because the native speaker captures their emotional reading soul, where the nonnative speaker captures nothing. If we take the time to help nonnative speakers develop an appreciation for the rhythms and nuances of English, I believe it will serve them well throughout their educational and professional lives.

To this end I always spend as much time as I can on description and narration, and unlike many of my colleagues, I emphasize it even at the advanced levels. I start out by examining parts of speech because good description relies on the use of powerful verbs, adjectives, and adverbs. (How many students use the same verbs over and over? And how many still confuse what adjectives and adverbs do or how they are to be used?) I also focus on the five senses and have students explore these physically and then in writing. Finally, I cover figurative language. I've placed tiger balm on foreheads for hot/cold sensations, taken blind walks, brought in an old conehead skull, given Rorschach psychological writing tests, listened to songs and read poems using cloze exercises—songs like James Taylor's "Sweet Potato Pie," or poems like Frost's "A Dust of Snow."

I also teach creative writing. One of my favorite units, on Edgar Lee Masters's *Spoon River Anthology* (1920), enables students to tap into the lives of people who at first might not seem to have much in common with them—but as the students read and then later begin to write, they realize that we all are really similar. The people of Spoon River were either very bitter or joyful about their lives in relationship to each other in their small town, and this is what makes their poems so powerful. Listen to how Masters begins the poem of Amanda Barker, speaking from the grave where she and the other characters of the book are buried:

Henry got me with child

Knowing that I could not bring forth life

Without losing my own.

(Masters, 1920 p. 31)

Now just imagine what the rest of her song is about, and what Henry has to say in his song from the grave!

In class we read selections like this from the anthology, I show my slides of the river, and we talk about this part of the Midwest, where I spent a decade and used to go tubing down the meandering Spoon. Then I turn the tables and have the students create their own anthology. I create the personas of a number of fictional characters equal to the number of students in the class. I give the students the name and a brief description of a fictional character: Max Stewart, a town barber who dies mysteriously in a fire along with Maybell Pearson, his lover (this persona given to another student). Maybell's husband, Drew (again this persona given to another student), was a ruthless landowner who was later hanged for killing a man. Then I have them each create a poem. What makes this so great is that students are speaking from the dead one last time, one last chance to get life's troubles off their chests. And students are speaking about *each other* since the fictional characters all lived in the same town. Where one writer may say nice things about a person, the one written nicely about may really rip into the other. (Ron Balsamo)

Through reading and writing in Ron's classes, students from all over the world can go to Spoon River, live and die there, creating a self who remains part of the community.

Many instructors in middle schools, high schools, and colleges use poetry as an important written genre with ESL students. Describe your experiences with poetry in the classroom. What have you observed in others' classes and/or how have you used poetry in your own classroom teaching?

In my jaunts into teaching creative writing, my students travel all over the world by reading travel literature. I've taken several groups of students across the United States with Andrei Codrescu in his bright red *Road Scholar* (1993) Cadillac, awed by his experience of immigrating to the United States as a young adult and by his insights into Americans and our values, especially freedom. We've gone to Mexico with Mary Morris (1988), to India with Pico Iyer (1988), and to New York City with Eva Hoffman (1989). (See the bibliography for references to these terrific works by Codrescu, Hoffman, Iyer, and Morris. Regardless of whether you use them in your teaching, they're great reads!)

When my students begin to dabble in creating their own travel writing through assignments in my class they relive favorite places and moments, and they reexamine themselves along the way. I have always taught travel writing with a student population of both native and nonnative speakers of English. Like Ron Balsamo, I have seen my nonnative students excel in comparison to their native classmates in this course. They bring much more relevant experience to bear on the cultural reflections and self-analysis that emerge from travel writing as a genre.

Lucy Calkins (1994) tells of a high school creative writer:

Morat is an avid mystery reader, so his teacher, Rose Napoli, wisely encouraged him to try his hand at writing mysteries. After he'd written a page of his story, Morat explained to [Calkins] that he was including "fake clues." He said, "I want to fool the readers, to give them the wrong ideas so the ending is a surprise." He added, "In the book I'm reading, that's what the guy did." Morat also decided not to put much description into his story because he figured the kids would skip it or get bored, just as he does with similar passages in his reading book. Once Morat looked up from his reading and said, "I'm better at titles than this author is. It is pretty stupid how he calls this book *Mystery of the Silent Friends* when they talk all the time." (Calkins, 1994, p. 280)

Calkins goes on to reflect on Morat's writing strategies:

Morat is able to apprentice himself to the author of *Mystery of the Silent Friends* not only because both he and his mentor are working within similar genres, but also and more primarily, because Morat believes that he is a writer of literature. In order for Morat to deliberately adopt the strategies he sees his mentor using, Morat first needs to know that he, like his mentor, is crafting a piece of real literature that will be read by real readers. (ibid.)

Bringing the entertainment of text (reading and writing) to our students as a means of facilitating their language acquisition is what teaching creative writing is about. At any proficiency level, there may be places in the curriculum where reading literature and writing creatively may provide breadth and interest to the program. I have taught required EAP writing courses at enough institutions to know how difficult it can be to fit this type of work into academic course syllabi. But in elective college courses, in high school courses, or in any array of nonacademic programs, creative writing can give students and teachers great pleasure.

The most immediate benefit to students of courses in travel literature that I have taught is the inspiration they enjoy from the readings. Who doesn't get inspired by a good autobiography or adventure? Admittedly, literature written in Elizabethan English may well come across to ESL students as distant from the English-speaking culture they are experiencing. But by choosing literature in the ways that Melinda Erickson discussed (see pp. 21-2), you as the ESL writing teacher will appeal to your students. How can you do otherwise? Good literature has universal appeal. The inspiration many ESL students experience from travel literature or immigrant literature can lead to an intrinsic motivation for writing. In other words, rather than writing because of an extrinsic motivation such as grades or course requirements, your ESL students write from intrinsic motivation—the excitement they get from putting their ideas down on paper.

I began this chapter mentioning an ESL student of mine who praised the freedom she felt doing nonexpository creative writing in English. Leki and Carson (1997, p. 50) also found that students called writing without regard to a source text *freeing*, as compared to writing from sources—as long as the students were familiar with the topic, that is. In having my students recreate their memories of travel and special locations in English, I find they have lots to say on paper, and they love the process of creating their stories. They spend far more time on their travel writing assignments than they had expected to because they enjoy the writing so much that they keep returning again and again to each project. (Talk about motivation!) And they astound even themselves that they write as much as they do. The sense of accomplishment for these students is deeper and more internal than when they turn in an academic exposition because of the personal nature of what they reveal in their creative writing.

It is after experiencing the satisfaction of that accomplishment that my creative writing students have felt that reading and writing in English can actually become a part of their psyches. They still grapple with the text they are creating, bumbling along trying to get it to work, just as they do when writing more restricted expository discourse. But the process of writing creatively seems more often to give students a new self-identity, just as it did Eva Hoffman, who discovered a new self-identity as a writer of the English language.

---

1 *An entree into creative writing can be through sensory descriptions. Take a look at the first chapter of Steinbeck's* Cannery Row *(1945). It's chock full of vivid descriptions of sounds, smells, and sights. I think it's great to get my ESL writing students in Monterey inspired by Steinbeck's wonderful description, then for them to go down to Cannery Row itself to experience it decades later— and then, of course, to write about it.*

What is a good book written about a location near you, one that you could use with students to elicit descriptive pieces of writing? If you can't think of a book, then go right to the location—where could your students go to experience and collect sensory details to use in descriptive writing? What could you have them write?

---

2 *Following is an excerpt from Andrei Codrescu's* Road Scholar. *This passage invariably sparks energy—my ESL students always nod knowingly and respond with similar experiences. How would you use the excerpt in a writing course? With classmates or colleagues, decide on a student group and course type; then design a writing project around the Codrescu piece.*

> My life would have been much simpler, I think, if I had learned how to drive when I came to America. An American without a car is a sick creature, a snail that has lost its shell. Living without a car is the worst form of destitution, more shameful by far than not having a home. A carless person is a stationary object, a prisoner, not really a grownup. A homeless person, by contrast, may be an adventurer, a vagabond, a lover of the open sky. The only form of identification an American needs is a driver's license.
>
> Time and time again I stood humiliated before a bank clerk who would not admit to my existence because a passport meant nothing to her. Over and over I've had to prove my existence to

petty clerks and policemen for whom there was only one valid form of ID. Driven to despair, I wrote my first autobiography, *The Life and Times of an Involuntary Genius,* at age twenty-three for the sole reason of having my picture on the cover. Whenever a banker asked to see "some identification," I pulled the book from my mirrored Peruvian bag and pointed to the cover. More often than not, it was not enough. "What we mean is," the flustered interpreters of rules and upholders of reality would insist, "we want to see some *proper* ID!" Books have never been proper to those in charge of upholding the status quo.

One very late night in California my friend Jeffrey Miller and I got lost on a country road somewhere above the Pacific Ocean. The sky was pierced by so many stars we thought we were on a cosmic stage with the ocean roaring below us. We stopped because we were tired and awed. Suddenly, the lights of something unearthly and huge were upon us. It was a California Highway Patrol cruiser, its blue light flashing. Jeff stopped slowly, as if he were reluctant to surrender to the intense light, which might be an alien craft. The officer asked Jeff for his ID, which my friend fished with some difficulty either from the depths of his fascinating glove compartment, which was his portable office, or from one of his pockets, which was equally cluttered with napkins full of poetry, pencil nubs, lucky stones, and, undoubtedly, Ritz crackers in case of shipwreck. Jeffrey believed every journey was final, and that one must be prepared.

The officer then turned to me. "Your license!" "I don't drive," I said. He heard that. He also heard the foreign "r" in the word "drive," and was alerted to the possibility of a potential illegal alien. I pulled out my book. "I wrote this. See, that's my picture!" The cop took the book back to his cruiser and started reading. He read and read. Eons passed. The stars in the sky changed. Jeff and I slept and woke, grew old, died, and came back. At long last, the officer returned from the deeps of time, and tapped my face on the cover with a thoughtful trigger finger. "Anybody can fake a pitcher like this!" he said. "If they could," I argued wearily, "would they bother to write a book to go with it?" "It's OK," he said, *"this time!"* Well, it was OK that time, and Jeff and I went on our way. I immediately wrote another autobiography, for that California cop. In that book, called *In America's Shoes,* which also sports my face on the cover, I told the above story—just in case we met again.

My adventures in the land of those without drivers' IDs would fill several books. Lost souls live in that world: illegal aliens, space aliens, the crazy, the stubborn, handicapped pedestrians of every stripe. The truth is that an American without a driver's license doesn't have an identity. (Codrescu, 1993, pp. 3-4)

3 *Explain your group's writing project from # 2, above, to other classmates and colleagues. Have them analyze your plans following the guidelines in Chapter 3, investigation #4 (pp. 34-35).*

Suggested Readings

Sometimes writing teachers need coaching from other writers in ways to get creative juices flowing, especially in preparation for incorporating creative writing into a course curriculum. Many people's favorite coach these days seems to be Natalie Goldberg. She's written several helpful books, in particular, *Writing Down the Bones: Freeing the Writer Within* (1986). Another favorite of many over the years has been Peter Elbow, especially his *Writing with Power* (1981). And for those of you who still like to curl up with Ray Bradbury's *The Martian Chronicles* (1950), as I do, take a look at his *Zen in the Art of Writing* (1990).

For those of you who want less coaching and more practical writing tasks that will help you, as well as your students, become more creative writers, see Barbara Danish's *Writing as a Second Language: A Workbook for Writing and Teaching Writing* (1981). Her exercises can be adapted for use with adolescent and adult ESL student writers.

If you're interested in the sociolinguistic question of nonnative speakers of English appropriating the English language while still maintaining a sociocultural mindset of the people of their native language, read Chapter 8 of Maybin and Mercer's *Using English: From Conversation to Canon* (1996).

5

INTEGRATING WRITING INTO THE MULTISKILLS COURSE WITH COMPUTERS

In the sentiment of writing across the curriculum, I regard teaching writing as everybody's job. All language teachers teach writing, even those teachers who work with integrated skills classes. Your course title doesn't have to spell out the word *writing* for you to be teaching exactly that. Likewise, you don't need to have the word *computer* in your course title to build technology into your students' classroom language-learning experience. Let's take a look at a multiskills class with ESL students grappling with electronic text.

Rona Nashiro Koe teaches ESL at the University of California at Santa Barbara. The students in her lower-level integrated skills ESL course meet in a traditional classroom most of the time, and sometimes in the school computer lab. In the computer lab they do a lot of work at the computers with electronic mail and with the World-Wide Web.

In bringing computers into her ESL course curricula, Rona uses lots of learner training and builds time in for making the transition from paper to computer. Initially she has students e-mail homework assignments to her whenever an assignment allows for it. She also has students keep informal journals on e-mail, sometimes writing extemporaneously on topics Rona has assigned; more often writing freely, journal-style, on their own.

Merely submitting homework and journals by e-mail is enough computer contact to make some students feel nervous. Rona works with students who have never seen a keyboard before, and for whom working at a computer can be extremely anxiety-producing. After some time, individual attention, and encouragement, Rona is able to move these students, initially threatened by the computer work, ahead with the majority of her students. Most of Rona's students love doing assignments by e-mail because, as they tell her, they can type faster than they can write.

Once her students are familiar with e-mail, Rona facilitates a pen-pal system that allows each student to write to another in the class. They write informal short letters, ask and answer questions, initiate and follow up on topics, and basically reinforce spoken language practice from the classroom. Rona gives them feedback once each student electronically forwards to her copies of the memos and responses. She has also expanded this type of communication to a pen-pal system with students in a class taught by a colleague in another school. Rona suggests that writing to a pen-pal (or *com-pal*, for computer pen-pal) is a good way to begin sending e-mail to someone other than the teacher.

At this point in Rona's course she brings in activities and tasks that get her students writing on the computer and using English in various ways. There are probably as many versions of chain story activities out there as there are language teachers. And rightly so, given the useful ways they integrate writing with reading. Rona has managed a nice spin on chain stories by having a student in the computer lab write the beginning of a story, say the first two or three lines, and then e-mail it to the person sitting to his or her right. That student checks his or her e-mail, reads how far along the story is, adds two or three lines, and e-mails the entire emerging story to the person sitting to his or her right, and so on. Over time, while the class engages in other activities in the computer lab, the story develops. Everybody loves the story in the end, especially his or her own contribution.

Once Rona took her ESL students to a movie—it turned out to be one of those teaching adventures in which plans are foiled, you make do, and then your students turn it into something better than you had ever imagined. In Rona's case the power went off up and down the street the movie theater was on, so the class only saw the first half hour or so of the movie. At least everybody had seen the time and place of the setting, the main characters, and the story's situation and conflict. So Rona turned the movie—what she thought was going to provide lots of listening practice—into a writing task, asking the students to write "summaries" of the movie, predicting the story line and what happened to each of the main characters. Because they had been studying past tenses, the students were to write their stories in the past tense. Each student e-mailed a story to another classmate, who was assigned to edit the verb tenses. The editor wrote suggestions in capital letters immediately after the incorrect wording and e-mailed the story back so that the writer could see where and how to consider improving things. Then the edited story was e-mailed to Rona for her feedback. During the sequence of activities the students used English creatively, communicatively, and purposefully. Writing and computer use were integrated into the task in a natural way.

Besides writing via e-mail, Rona has her ESL students use English on the Internet. In introducing the World-Wide Web to her students, Rona teaches them the vocabulary and kinesics of basic computer search skills. As she says, it's a matter of "click here, click there, type in a word there, click, click, click." Then, in groups, Rona's students brainstorm topics they're interested in looking up on the Web—the wider the range of possible topics, the better. Next they're ready to get on the Web and look around, with a task of finding one interesting Web site and printing it. In a following class session, Rona's students present their Web sites to the class, impressing each other with the breadth of on-line information that can be tapped from cyberspace.

That type of initiation to the Web can take place with students searching and clicking on the various graphics and points of information on the screen. Next, Rona has her students find Web sites by using Web addresses (also known as uniform resource locators, or URLs), which require short but perfect bits of writing. With these computer skills, Rona's students are free to carry out tasks such as previewing or reviewing movies: finding on-line movie clips or interviews with famous entertainers, listening over and over, and talking and writing about them. Another favorite group project is to "plan a trip" by accessing

Internet information on tourism for the location, sights, hotels, restaurants, camping, hiking, whatever. This is great for lower-level students, says Rona, because the reading is simple (prices, dates, place names, maps, advertisements) and the writing straightforward (e-mail messages requesting information, addresses). As a source of advertisements and entertainment, the Web gives us very useful authentic text in English.

Rona admits that the road to writing can get rocky in the electronic classroom. She cites continuing difficulties with some students who are not familiar with a keyboard or with using computers. Getting things like passwords and account numbers exactly right can be a hassle, and the computer can grow into a monolithic technical hurdle. Rona is concerned about effects of such technology biasing, wondering whether these students might become too frustrated to get their best ideas into writing, might write less than they would with pen and paper, or might just be unable to see the writing for all the technological hassles. Another problem for the students and teacher in an electronic classroom is the possibility of a student's completed assignment getting lost or "going to e-mail heaven," as Rona and her students say. Just as there are myriad reasons a student may not have written homework to turn in, so it is for computer assignments. Rona suggests having students print a hard copy of assignments before trying to e-mail them to the teacher, at least until most of the kinks in technical transmission are ironed out.

By using the computer to carry out language-learning tasks, ESL students in multiskills classes can potentially improve both their English language and their computer literacy. The writing done in these contexts is authentic text being sent to real live audiences, who are actually sending replies.

In many countries in the world computer literacy is now part of what we as language teachers are responsible for teaching. The computer replaces pen and paper as a tool for making text, and our language courses eventually follow. In many ways Rona's multiskills ESL course is much like any number of communicative language courses, except that the text the students are reading and the writing they are producing is electronic. By studying in a computer classroom, language learners become empowered linguistically and technologically, gaining useful knowledge for job-hunting and careers.

Another avenue for language practice for our students with access to computers can be e-mail mailing-list programs, which are electronic bulk mail information sources students can subscribe to. Many of these are discussion groups your students can either eavesdrop on, which is a great way to learn, or enter into conversation with. For example, <EST-SL listserv@asuvm.inre.asu.edu> is the address for an ESL student on-line discussion group, complete with teachers offering advice on scientific and technical writing.

Unfortunately in middle schools and high schools across the United States, there are computers that sit dormant in classrooms and computer labs. I know from experience in a number of school settings that the computer hardware was funded, but teacher or student training in the use of the hardware or accompanying software was not. Many of my fellow teaching colleagues who are knowledgeable about computer use in language teaching became so by training themselves. If you happen to have the opportunity to take a course or workshop in this area, by all means do so—inform yourself! It is the responsibility of all of us as language teachers to make the best use of whatever teaching tools are available. The dormant computers that sit in our classrooms today will awaken with the new millenium, and you, as a responsible teacher, need to be there to help students use computers as tools of the time for interacting with text.

Reading and writing are authentic tasks when there is an actual audience besides the language teacher. The computer e-mail capacity enables teachers to manage individual pen-pals for a whole language class so that students can send and receive pen-pal correspondence far more frequently than via paper mail. The Internet provides a rich source of authentic language. These resources are becoming widely accessible, making computers instrumental, in at least two senses, for writing and language learning.

---

1 *Investigate information on the Internet that might be useful to your students:*

- Chat rooms, idiom pages, graffitti pages, etc., for ESL students
  <http://www.eslcafe.com>

- The American Studies Web
  <http://www.cis.yale.edu/~david;/amstud.html>

- Periodicals, magazines, and journals
  Gopher:
  Host: ftp.std.com, Port: 70, Select: 1/periodicals
  WWW:
  gopher://ftp.std.com:70/11/periodicals

- The Library of Congress
  <http://lcweb.loc.gov/>

What else can you find? Copy Web sites and bring them in for "show and tell."

---

2 *One time I sat in on a multiskills ESL course held in a multimedia computer center on the campus of the Monterey Institute of International Studies. The team teachers, Susan Ando and Leila Najm, organized the course around creating homepages. On the day, I visited some students were learning how to add scanned photos and others were learning how to add sound to their homepages. The classroom language use by the students was quite astounding, and by the instructors was minimal. Especially impressive was the students' written language, which was being honed for the final copy for their homepages. It was a terrific course!*

Call around to see if you can observe classroom interaction in a computer learning situation. Try to find an electronic ESL class, a computer workshop for ESL students, or a computer lab that ESL writing students may use. Take note of the authenticity of the classroom language use, student involvement and collaboration, and the teacher's role. How effective did you find the class session?

Suggested Readings

If you need a nudge to step into the world of computers as pedagogical tools, read Janet Schofield's depiction of an urban secondary school and how computer technology fits in, and sometimes doesn't, *Computers and Classroom Culture* (1995).

For an analysis of computer use in schools and the lack of use of many computers out there in the schools, take a look at *Computers and Cultural Diversity* (1991) by DeVillar and Faltis. They propose more cooperative and collaborative teaching and learning in the schools, supported by computer technology for tutoring and student research.

A helpful how-to book for instructors is Mark Warschauer's *E-Mail for English Teaching: Bringing the Internet and Computer Learning Networks into the Language Classroom* (1996). Particularly useful for instructors are resource lists of organizations, journals, and electronic bulletin boards.

Sample student handbooks for using e-mail and the Internet are Carol Clark's *A Student's Guide to the Internet* (1996); Crump and Carbone's *English Online: A Student's Guide to the Internet and World Wide Web* (1997); and Mark Warschauer's *E-Mail for English Teaching* (1996).

On-line Sources

Keep up with the teaching field by Internet with these professional journals:

Teaching English as a Second Language Electronic Journal (TESL-EJ)
<http://www-writing.berkeley.edu/TESL-EJ/ej01/toc.html>

Kairos: A Journal for Teachers of Writing in Webbed Environments
<http://english.ttu.edu/kairos/>

Resources for Writers and Writing Instructors
<http:/www.english.upenn.edu/~jlynch/writing.html>

The following are e-mail mailing-list programs your ESL students can subscribe to:

English for Science and Technology
<EST-SL listserv@asuvm.inre.asu.edu>

Online Writing Centers and Resources
<http://kramer.ume.maine.edu/~wcenter/others.html>

In case you're interested in traditional writing resources now on-line:

Elements of Style by William Strunk, Jr.
<http://www.columbia.edu/acis/bartleby/strunk/>

Roget's Thesaurus
<http://humanities.uchicago.edu/forms_unrest/ROGET.html>

Webster's Revised Unabridged Dictionary
<http://humanities.uchicago.edu/forms_unrest/webster.form.html>

6

GETTING STUDENTS
TO REVIEW
EACH OTHER'S DRAFTS

There are certain days during any term when my academic writing classroom becomes a workshop. I arrange things ahead of time through homework assignments, worksheets, posted agendas of tasks, posted guidelines, and anything else I can think of to set up class sessions in which I step back into the shadows to get the students collaborating in productive ways.

Here's what you might see if you walked in on a day when students are collaborating on in-progress drafts, offering each other advice for revision.

Near the blackboard a piece of construction paper with five points is posted:

- Take out your peer review sheet, the original assignment sheet for this paper, and your partner's draft.

- These are ROUGH drafts. Give kind, helpful, and specific comments.

- For each writer's paper, talk about each point on the peer review sheet.

- Make lots of suggestions about HOW to improve (not only WHAT to improve).

- TAKE NOTES to remember your partner's advice.

On one wall many photocopied sheets of paper are posted, each with an excerpt marked, a question handwritten in the margin, and a piece of paper posted underneath, some blank and some with brief handwritten comments. The excerpts are from drafts of the students' papers, with each student writer's question for class comment: "What readings will support my idea here?" "Does this example from my own life help to explain my point?" "What else can I say in my conclusion?" Three students are standing at that wall, each looking at a different excerpt. Two students are reading, and the third is writing something on the blank piece of paper underneath the photocopied excerpt.

On the blackboard, the class session's agenda is written:

10:00   Begin peer review groups; Free moment?
         Comment on the wall!
10:50 (or so)   10-minute break.
11:20 (or so)   Finish up groups and make comments
         on the wall.
11:35   Whole class discussion of how papers are going.
11:50   Take your own page & comments from the wall.
         Revise lots over the weekend! Individual
         conferences next week. Bye-bye!

Each student has a green peer review sheet and a green assignment sheet that look like this:

REVISION GUIDE

Read once quickly through the entire paper; then reread again more carefully and make notes on each of the following questions. Use your notes during discussion with your partner in class next time.

1. Reread the introductory paragraph(s). Do they give you an idea of what the whole paper is going to be about (U.S. immigration policy, minority/immigrant groups, etc.)? Do they make you want to continue reading? Do they define key terms and issues clearly? <u>What suggestions do you have for (drafting or) improving the introductory paragraphs?</u>

2. Is there a clearly stated thesis (in other words, a position or claim about U.S. policy on immigration) that ties the whole paper together? <u>How can the thesis be specified or clarified to improve the way it ties the paper together?</u> Review the paper once more to look for ideas that do not relate closely to the thesis. <u>Suggest places that should be revised or deleted in order to fit better with the overall thesis.</u>

3. Think about the organization of the paper. Are the paragraphs well-developed? Are claims clearly stated and well-supported with evidence? Are paragraphs logically ordered? Suggest ways in which organization can be improved.

4. Reread the assigned topic from the green assignment sheet from Cherry. Are all the required aspects of the paper covered? Suggest ways the paper can more directly prove the writer's understanding of U.S. immigration policy as an international issue, or suggest ways the writer can make his/her perspective on this issue stronger in order to better address the assignment.

5. Has the writer made it clear which ideas and claims come from him/her and which ideas came from Rosen/ Skerry/Schrag or any other writer of background sources? Suggest places and words that would help improve the differentiation between the writer's ideas and those of background sources.

6. Reread the concluding paragraphs of the paper. Do they completely discuss the significance of the paper or the purpose of the paper? Remember, as an outside reader, it may be easier for you to think of ideas that could help here than the writer. Discuss ideas the writer can use to expand and strengthen his/her concluding paragraphs.

7. What do you think of the title? Does it reflect the thesis of this particular paper? Is it specific enough so that it could not be used for someone else's paper? Suggest ways to specify the title so that it more directly relates to the thesis of this particular paper. (If there is no title yet, help the writer compose a good, specific one.)

ASSIGNMENT SHEET

TOPIC: Discuss U.S. immigration policy in terms of motivation and effects: compare and contrast various approaches to immigration policy from throughout U.S. history, including current policy issues. Also focus on a particular immigration policy, demonstrating its effect(s) or potential effect(s) on a particular immigrant or minority group in the U.S.

BACKGROUND READING: Articles by Rosen, Skerry, and Schrag (especially Rosen) in The New Republic issue of 30 Jan. '95. If you find it helpful, you might use the periodical search facilities in the library to find a more recent newspaper or magazine article on this issue; however, this is not required.

GETTING STARTED: Study the Rosen, Skerry, and Schrag articles, taking notes on U.S. immigration policies, their motivations (reasons/justifications), their effects on the U.S. population at large, and their effects on particular immigrant and minority groups (e.g., Japanese, Thais, Tibetans, African-Americans, women, etc.).

DUE DATES:

T 1/31	Exchange rough drafts with classmates. (Bring one copy of your paper to class.)
Th 2/3	Critique each other's papers in class.
T 2/7	Revised draft of paper due to Cherry for her comments.
Th 2/9	Individual conferences with Cherry on your paper.
T 2/14	Bring newly revised draft to class for proofreading.
Th 2/16	Final draft due for a grade.

EVALUATION CRITERIA:

■ Introductory paragraph(s) previewing your entire paper;

■ Clearly stated overall thesis, tying all of your ideas together;

■ Specific title, related to your thesis;

■ Organization (logically ordered, well-developed paragraphs with claims supported by evidence);

■ Clear differentiation between your ideas and those of any other authors;

■ Concluding paragraph(s) discussing the significance of the ideas you have discussed in a well-developed manner;

■ Appropriate grammar, mechanics, word usage, spelling, etc.

If you came in near the beginning of the class session you would usually see me standing in a corner of the room watching and listening. I gauge my activities during the class period according to what I see and hear happening throughout, but especially near the beginning, as things get rolling. If I see that some students have very little writing so far in draft form, I know I will approach each individually during the second hour of class to ask how it's going, what they're going to do next to get more written, and whether they'd like to see me later in the day for more individual help.

For the moment, I see a student sitting silently with a group, looking out the window. I walk over in that direction and stop on the way to point out to another student that he needs the green peer review sheet, not the yellow peer review sheet we used for the last paper. He shuffles in his notebook and pulls out the green sheet. I go on over to the daydreamer, do a deep-knee bend, and look evenly into the student's face.

"How's your draft coming along?"

"Okay. I wait for Estevan. He read my paper."

"Great. Have you decided on the main thing you're going to say in your paper? What's important for immigration reform?"

"Maybe family in United States. And I think freedom."

"What do you mean, freedom?"

I pull over an empty chair and sit. For a couple of minutes the student talks generally about freedom, mainly praising freedom, and about the fact that many immigrants have extended families in the United States. I listen and nod encouragement. I ask a question that paraphrases the essay topic: "If you could change the U.S. immigration law, what would you say about freedom? And what would you say about an immigrant who has family in the U.S.?" The student hesitates. I add, "Why don't you think about that until Estevan finishes with Akiko, and write down some notes to yourself?" I leave, taking a mental note that I need to continue helping that student focus on paper topics.

I hover in another corner of the room so I can see what's happening in the groups from a different angle. I approach another silent student sitting near a group.

Again my deep-knee bend and opener: "How's your draft so far?"

"Fine." The student looks away.

I move down a little further, hoping it offers the student more power to be looking down at me. "Have you come up with a main idea for your paper, Naoko? Something important about how to improve immigration law?"

"I'm still working on it." No eye contact.

"How about if you tell me about it next week after you've worked more on it?"

"Yes."

"Take notes on what your partner says, okay? So you've got lots of ideas written down for when you work more on it over the weekend. Sound all right?"

"Yes."

"What are you going to work on right now until your partner's free?" Naoko looks down at me blankly. I look over at the wall with the posted excerpts.

"I'll read paragraphs," she says with determination, pointing at the wall. I smile. "This is a hard paper, Naoko." She looks away, smiles, and nods. "Are you also working on papers for your other classes?"

"No. But I have oral presentation tomorrow."

"In what class? What's it about?"

"For environmental econ. On the green revolution in India."

"How's it coming along?"

"Okay. I have appointment today with my public speaking teacher."

"Great! I hope she can help you. And do you know that Kenji wrote a paper last semester on the green revolution? Maybe he can help. Okay, well . . ." We both stand and I nod at the excerpts on the wall. "Maybe you'll see an approach that will help you in your immigration paper."

I stroll across the room to another group, eavesdropping the entire way. I linger for a moment over the group until there's a juncture in the conversation for me to ask how it's going. They show me a *New York Times* article and ask me what a particular sentence means. I explain briefly and ask how that might help their papers. They look at each other and agree that it wouldn't help after all, but maybe they'll find something else in there somewhere. I praise them for being careful about selecting only information from the newspaper article if the information supports the ideas they are writing about. I ask them if I can borrow the article for a moment to write the citation on the board for the other students. As I leave the blackboard, I pass by my pile of stuff and grab a yellow sticky note to remind myself to check with Naoko how her paper's going early next week.

At the wall with the posted excerpts I see a student has posted the last paragraph of his draft with the request "What else can I say in my conclusion?" I go over to the student and suggest it might be difficult for students to give helpful comments to his question without reading the rest of the draft of his paper. He nods sheepishly. I say I'd be interested in helping him on his conclusion. Would he like to talk about it now, or after he's revised some more? We make an appointment for next week. And so on.

For me as the teacher, peer review sessions offer time in the classroom to check in with individual students to help me consider how I can best help them in later private conferences. It has been suggested elsewhere that peer review becomes most successful if it is integrated into the writing course, so that from the beginning of the term students are aware of writing for peers as well as teacher audiences (Mittan, 1989). In my own writing courses the curricular integration is strongest between peer review and conferencing. They play off each other, providing mutual reinforcement. Individual conferences end up being more successful when I can prepare to follow up on issues with particular students, issues I am alerted to during peer review sessions. Occasionally a student may question the legitimacy of peer comments, wanting to rely more on teacher comments. I am always able to remind such a peer review skeptic that individual conferences with me are just around the corner, and that in the meantime he or she can consider whether to incorporate the classmate's suggestions. In this way the interplay between peer review and conferencing helps students who rely on teacher feedback to develop autonomy as writers. For all of my students, peer review sessions followed a couple of days later by individual conferences with me end up encouraging significant revision of ideas and organization.

Besides encouraging revision, I agree with writing process proponents who use peer review sessions for other pedagogical reasons. For example, peer review helps students write for audiences besides just the teacher. I find that, quite often, a peer reviewer can ask enough questions or express enough confusion that a classmate is able to push an early draft of what Flower coined *writer-based prose* to *reader-based prose* by the time I see the draft at the time of a conference (Flower, 1989). Also, and very importantly, peer review provides a means of getting more feedback to student writers on drafts than I possibly have time to offer. Students offer each other input on ways to approach the assignment or use background sources that I might never even have thought of.

I agree with Mittan (1989) that peer review guidelines or worksheets are most effective when they are topic-based, with questions based on the particular writing topic the students are writing about. In other ways, however, my peer review sheets vary from those other teachers use. Mittan and others pose questions or tasks on their peer review sheets based on general principles of responding to writing. For example, what do you enjoy most about the paper? What do you see as the purpose and audience of the paper? What are questions you have about the paper? What suggestions can you offer the writer? Although I find this type of response encouraging and effective in conferences or written on final drafts, I find it more important at the peer review stage early in the revision process to focus students' attention on the criteria for final evaluation. When students are informed right along with the original assignment how they will be graded and then are reminded of the grading criteria while doing revising and peer critiquing, they never complain that they didn't know what was expected of them in their papers.

Another aspect of my peer review sessions that varies from a number of other writing instructors, is my means of determining partners to review each other's papers. Advocates of collaborative learning often think in terms of optimal numbers of participants in a group, usually arriving at four or five peers for each group to allow for plenty of collaboration and input. Others working with ESL writers suggest mixing students by first-language background (Hafernik, 1983). Still others assign pairs according to students' writing strengths (Mittan, 1989). I find, however, that students offer more specific feedback if they are grouped with peers according to the content of their papers. After the initial peer review session of the term, when I allow students to select their own partners, I arrange groups such that students work with partners whose papers focus on the assigned topic in a similar way, or whose background sources are the same, or, if given a choice of topics, who have selected the same or similar writing topics. In such cases students are better prepared to become more deeply involved in the discussion of ideas, argument development, use of background sources, and other areas of a draft that usually require substantive revision.

Groups of three, with each student reading two papers but responding to questions on the peer review sheet for just one of the two papers, seem to work well in my classroom. In this way each student has seen more than one other draft and benefited from the extra input, but for homework is only required to prepare explanations to the peer review worksheet for one other student. Two students talk together at any given time. Some students are able to gain helpful insight by listening to the discussion between the other two in the group of three; others end up working more on their own papers during those few minutes.

In my peer review sessions there is always the other peer review task as well: to look at the excerpts students have chosen to post on the wall with requests for specific feedback from others. Many students choose to do that during the time when their group partners are working together. I find the one-on-one discussion between pairs of students ends up focusing quite nicely on the paper, the topic, the ideas and organization, and on ways to revise, more so than discussions among larger groups. With more group participants the focus of the talk becomes more one of fast-paced consensus-building, with the students dancing around the paper's ideas and topic while they place (or more often avoid placing) their various opinions in juxtaposition. As Carson and Nelson (1994) point out, students from collectivist cultures like Japan and the People's Republic of China (both highly represented in my writing classes) may care more about group harmony than advice for revision. It seems to me that pairs establish their own integrity more quickly than groups, and student comments appear straightforwardly directed at the paper's ideas and ways the writer can improve the approach to and organization of those ideas through revision.

During peer review sessions in my classroom the students discuss their own and another's paper in depth, they examine and give brief written comments to excerpts from many other students in the class, and they usually have a brief chat with me. My role is one of facilitator, troubleshooter, and consultant to individuals during the actual peer review session. My preparation for and follow-up to peer review sessions is important (preparing the peer review sheet to correspond to the original assignment sheet, keeping track of struggles and accomplishments of individual students for conference discussion). But most important is that the students become deeply engaged in the content of their papers and that they revise extensively.

---

1 *Peer review does not work well unless it is orchestrated carefully. Think about one of the writing projects you developed from "investigations" sections in earlier chapters. Remind yourself for what student level and course type you were planning your writing assignment.*

Plan detailed steps you would follow in setting up a peer-review activity for that writing project with those students. If you would use a peer-review sheet, what would it look like? How would revision grow out of your activity?

---

2 *Imagine you are teaching a workshop-style class like mine, described earlier in this chapter. Let's say your traditional back-to-basics boss stops by, seeing you standing quietly by the wall watching your students. Your boss disapproves.*

Write a memo to your boss justifying the workshop atmosphere in which your students are reviewing each other's drafts.

---

3 *Find a classmate or colleague who, like you, is working on a term paper or some other important writing project. Practice your skills as writing coaches and peer collaborators by working with each other to determine areas in each of your drafts in which revision would help. Discuss strategies to try to make the best revision happen. You might consider the following factors:*

a. Review the professor's assignment together. If this is not a term paper, consider whatever instructions for the project are available. What areas of this draft could be expanded to address the assignment more completely? Discuss options for expanding those areas of the draft.

b. Are there evaluation criteria explicitly stated by the professor (or supervisor)? If so, review these criteria and determine what can be done in revising this draft (and how this can be done) to improve the final draft. If no evaluation criteria are stated explicitly, determine for yourselves the level of professionalism you will work toward on this paper. Then discuss ways to revise to make the quality of this draft that professional.

c. How well supported is the writing? Look for places in which the writer makes claims—is evidence provided for each claim that is made throughout the paper? Is the evidence appropriate for the claim in each case? Can you think of further evidence that can be added? (In other words, who else has made supporting claims or conducted relevant research?) Does the evidence given in each case provide enough support for the strength of the claim (e.g., radical claims require more over-whelming evidence than conservative claims).

d. And what about the claims themselves? Can they be restated in stronger, more specific ways? Can they be emphasized more? Has the writer given the impression that his or her claims are the most important ideas in the paper, or does it seem that the ideas of other people from the background sources have determined the direction of the paper? If the latter is the case (and assuming it is appropriate for the paper itself), discuss ways to better emphasize the writer's own ideas and claims so that the writer controls the direction of the paper more obviously.

e. Does the paper have some sort of overall coherence or unity? How can this be improved? Think about general focus, beginnings and endings, title, subtitles, and any other areas that might help unify the paper.

f. Does the paper end strongly? (Let's assume you want to avoid just having the paper fizzle at the end, giving the impression that you simply don't have anything else to say.) How can the ending be improved? Think about the paper as a whole and why it is significant—talk about that to generate ideas that might be worked into the concluding paragraphs or lines of the paper.

g. After you revise your papers further, what will you do next? Check with the professor or your supervisor about any questions you can't address? Get together again with each other to help each other proofread? Anything else you can think of?

Suggested Readings

The best treatments of writing workshop environments in middle and secondary schools come from Nancie Atwell's *In the Middle: Writing, Reading, and Learning with Adolescents* (1987) and Lucy McCormick Calkins's *The Art of Teaching Writing* (1994). I have been greatly inspired by both Atwell's and Calkins's work.

A number of important articles offer rationale and classroom ideas for peer review with ESL students at any level: Carson and Nelson (1994), Hafernik (1983), James (1981), Mittan (1989), and Stanley (1992).

For an interesting theoretical perspective on getting students to respond to each other's work, see Gere's *Writing Groups: History, Theory, and Implications* (1987).

7

RESPONDING TO THE WRITTEN WORK AND THE WRITER'S PROCESS

If only I had been paid by the hour all these years of teaching writing! I'd be a woman of means, retired from the university, living the good life of a travel writer. I'd go to Japan first, in April, for the cherry blossoms.

Sometimes while responding to a stack of student papers or going through one individual conference after another, I daydream. Sometimes I can be deciding how to guide the student to come up with a stronger conclusion and, in the same moment, I can be on the plane to Tokyo.

Writing teachers spend far more time reading and responding to student papers than any of us are comfortable 'fessing up to. What we need to do is organize ourselves and work toward more pay or release time for that extra layer of time that we invest in our students over and above what instructors of other courses in our schools do. Yes, we need to organize ourselves! I would, but I've got a stack of papers to read. . . .

When teaching a writing class I use a combination of conferencing, written comments on the drafts, and peer review. I usually try to conference on the first draft so that the writer and I can discuss the issues of audience and purpose. For the next written assignment, I try to conference on a second draft so that I can work with my students on other issues besides audience and purpose. I usually do peer review on at least one of the writing assignments. Of these, I think conferencing is the most effective tool for giving feedback to writers, since it is a negotiated process. However, conferencing for twenty minutes with twenty students is very time consuming. I probably spend an average of an hour per paper. I will say that of any class to teach, without a doubt writing is the most time-consuming, and I feel it should count as more teaching time. (Amy Tickle)

Amy Tickle teaches ESL writing at Michigan State University. Here she explains how she responds to papers her students are in the process of writing. Amy's focus in giving feedback differs according to how far along the student is in writing the paper—in other words, which draft the student is working on. "If it is the first draft, the first thing I look at is to ensure that I *and* the writer know what the purpose and audience of the paper are," says Amy. This understanding is the key to the rest of the rhetorical structure of the piece—and it is difficult to tap, says Amy, outside an in-person conference with the student. Once she knows what the purpose of the paper is, Amy reads the draft, looking at the ideas and content, evaluating everything for its overall relevance. Here's how Amy tells it:

> "What is the purpose of your paper?" Most of my students tend to look at me like I am a nutcase when we talk about the purpose of a paper. I think they come in expecting me to go through their entire paper and correct all the mistakes. Instead, they come in and I ask them what their purpose is, and sometimes it might take the whole twenty minutes just to get that straightened out. I think they probably walk away a lot of the times thinking that the conference was a big waste of time.

> But I do feel that most of my students "get it" by the end of the semester, and this becomes the most important thing they learn. I also explain to my students how I give feedback so they know why I am doing what I'm doing: what's the point of spending two hours grading a paper for grammar when none of it relates to the writer's intended purpose? I would say the majority of my students cannot identify a clear purpose when we meet for a conference on their first draft. But during the conference, we figure it out. I also find that if they are really able to determine their purpose, I tend to see a lot of major revisions (i.e., deleting large chunks of text, moving text to different places in the paper, adding completely new text, etc.) from the first to the second draft. It's like a lightbulb clicks on and they really see why the information does or doesn't belong.

> The second thing I usually do when responding in writing to a first draft is to indicate any places in the paper where I cannot understand the writer's meaning. Obviously this is important in order for me and the writer to determine if the content is appropriate!

> Once the writer has a clear purpose and audience, and the content in the paper is suitable for the purpose and audience, I move on to organizational features of the paper; for example, rhetorical style, like setting up a compare/contrast situation; whether some content might make better sense logically in a different part of the paper; whether the writer has split paragraphs appropriately and kept paragraphs unified; whether paragraphs have topic sentences; whether the writer has an effective introduction and a conclusion, etc.

> Once these issues are looked at, I give feedback on sentence level and mechanical issues. When looking at grammar, I first point out any sentences that totally impede meaning (as I mentioned before). At this stage I then try to look for patterns in the writers' grammatical errors. If I notice that they have many problems related to subject-verb agreement, then I may focus on that issue. I usually highlight several instances in the paper with that particular error and provide a grammatical explanation. Then I have the writer edit the rest of the paper for that error. I also have my students keep

"editing checklists" that are handed in with every paper so that I know what grammar points we have discussed and can check their papers for their progress with those points. It also keeps the editing task for the student less overwhelming.

So for any given conference, my comments depend on how far along the paper is. For example, if I get a first draft that has a clear purpose, all the content is relevant to the purpose, and there are no sentences from which I cannot ascertain the meaning, then I move on to look at the organizational issues. If those are fine, then I will proceed to sentence-level issues. Most important is writing purpose. My experience has shown that most writers have never thought about the purpose of their writing, and most therefore have little idea of what information they should include in the paper. Once they begin to understand this concept, I have found them to be better writers and also more excited about writing. (Amy Tickle)

Melinda Erickson (introduced in Chapter 3) also responds regularly to her students' writing and writing processes through individual conferences. She admits to being influenced by Goldstein and Conrad's (1990) article on the discourse pattern of negotiation during conferencing and its positive effect on revision. In order to encourage her students to take an active part in the conversation of the conference, negotiating the response to the draft, Melinda often remains silent. She waits for each student to talk about the draft and responds accordingly. Her silence gets her students to articulate their self-evaluative thoughts as they look for Melinda's confirmation or suggestions for alternative strategies. My guess is that Melinda's students, like Amy's, might leave a conference or two wondering what in the world was accomplished there. But, as Amy pointed out, by the end of the semester the students realize how much they learned about their own writing processes.

From much of their past experience in English classes, students come to our writing courses expecting to work on their grammar, spelling, and punctuation. They expect us as teachers to respond to those areas of their language use, even when we first want to focus on larger issues of composing before the sentence level.

Brainstorm ways to respond to students who want to work on grammar and mechanics rather than on composing. What can be done to bring students' and teachers' expectations in line?

RESPONDING TO CONTENT, RHETORIC, AND ORGANIZATION

Our students' expectations about the importance of sentence-level language issues often preoccupy them in the beginning stages of their drafting. In Chapter 2 we saw Kim work over each sentence with extreme care before moving on to the next sentence throughout his entire first draft (p. 9). That type of premature editing can curtail the student's development of ideas and content; or, as in

Kim's case, it can keep the student from focusing on anything other than a simple rhetorical approach or essay organization.

For these reasons it is important for second-language writing instructors to take clear-cut steps to respond to content, rhetoric, and organization in their students' writing, as Amy did. Amy's predictable question, "What's your purpose?" over time helps her students realize what it really means to accomplish something, to *say something,* in the writing. Other instructors focus more on their students' rhetorical approaches (for instance, how arguments are structured) influenced by contrastive issues discussed by Grabe and Kaplan (1996) and others. In my own teaching I focus on content most often when responding to my students' early drafts. I push my students to take ideas we've been reading and discussing and develop them in depth with accuracy, in order to avoid the pattern Leki and Carson (1997) point out of students writing clear, well-organized, but inaccurate ideas.

In working through any of these issues of content, rhetoric, and organization, the instructor needs to make an effort not to appropriate the students' writing (Sommers, 1984). It becomes much more a matter of learning what each student's intentions are and leading him or her to discover how to best get there, rather than giving suggestions about what to improve. How can this be done outside personal conferences? As Goldstein and Conrad (1990) explain, the more the student reiterates what the instructor has said in a conference, restating his or her understanding, rehearsing a new line of reasoning, the more likely the student is to make substantial revisions in following drafts.

RESPONDING TO SENTENCE-LEVEL ISSUES

Once content, rhetoric, and organization have been drafted and redrafted, it is important to move on to the sentence-level issues of grammar, spelling, and mechanics. As Amy does, many instructors delay discussing these smaller issues until the students' written ideas are in good shape. Just as Amy claims that one of the most important things her students learn is to write purposefully, for my students that most important thing may be the distinction between revising for content, rhetoric, and organization—primarily content—and editing or proofreading for sentence-level issues. Flatly refusing to discuss grammar "before its time" works badly, if at all. Instead, when students ask about sentence-level issues on early drafts, I enter into a brief conversation with them—in fact conducting a mini-lesson—and then I turn the tables back to content or approach, promising that improving grammar will be the most important thing to do once the ideas are in better shape. What every writing teacher knows is how important it is to be able to make immediate assessments of grammaticality and clear explanations of how to edit the language. I may not think of myself as a grammar teacher, but I have certainly taught far more grammar in individual writing conferences than even I will ever realize.

MEANS OF RESPONSE: ON PAPER, AUDIOTAPE, COMPUTER, AND CONFERENCING IN PERSON

Amy, Melinda, and I all prefer conferencing as a means of responding to students' drafts in progress. But we also all agree that the time conferencing demands is excessive. Life is too short, no question. Most writing instructors agree that responding briefly in the margins of student papers is one-sided, often not deciphered, and sometimes not even read, let alone used to make revisions. There's got to be a better way. Some instructors have tried giving feedback to students through editing programs on computer or audiotape. In both cases the instructor studies the student paper (either on screen or paper), marks places on the paper, and provides comments (either through typing editorial comments along the way or speaking into the tape recorder). The consensus is that the time spent giving responses to a whole class of students remains just about the same whether the instructor handwrites comments on the paper, types into an editing program, or talks into a cassette microphone, but in that same amount of time (more or less) the instructor is able to give a greater amount of advice, responding to more issues in depth on the computer or the tape player. A decision as to the means used for responding to student drafts is a situated decision, different for every teacher based on all of the intervening teaching circumstances. If your decision is for conferencing, the following eight "tips" may be helpful.

Tips for the ESL Writing Teacher on Conferencing

1. *Empower the student. Get the student to speak first and follow his or her agenda. Ask things like "How's the paper going?" and "What's giving you trouble at this point in the paper?" or be silent and wait for the student to begin talking.*

2. *Either read the whole paper prior to the conference or read sections of the paper that the student points out to you, rather than reading very small portions of text out of context.*

3. *Ask about the student's intended meaning before responding to specific sections ("What are you getting at here?" "Explain the main point of this part."). Depending on how your student answers, you may need to respond differently than you might first have expected. You'd be surprised how irrelevant your responses can be if you've assumed your student meant one thing but he or she really meant something else (a constant problem in giving only written feedback, sitting alone reading the stack of papers without any of the student writers there to talk to).*

4. *In responding to issues of content, approach, rhetoric, organization, etc., rather than telling the student how the paper should be, discuss what it is (analyze the discourse as a trained reader) and offer a number of alternatives, encouraging those the student responds to most positively. Suppress any desire to take over the paper or make it yours.*

5. *Keep checking to confirm that the student understands. Try to get the student to restate what he or she understands as a good way to improve sections of the paper. Encourage the student to take notes, or take notes for the student so he or she remembers what was discussed once it's time to sit down again to work on the paper.*

6. If it seems appropriate to discuss sentence-level language issues, respond by doing nitty-gritty pen-and-paper work. Model revision tactics on certain sections of the paper (perhaps regarding only one grammar/diction/mechanics point at a time), and then have the student do the same on another section of the paper.

7. Most important, be positive and encouraging, pointing out good aspects of the writing. . . .

8. At the same time, be realistic. If the paper needs to be revised greatly before it will be considered adequate according to the course standards, warn the student and be sure he or she leaves the conference with specific notes on alternative ways to proceed in the revision process. Arrange a follow-up appointment if necessary.

Remember Kim and June from Chapter 2? Here is their composition topic once again, followed by the papers each wrote. Study their papers, thinking about how you would respond to them.

Composition topic: Imagine that you are an anthropologist preparing to observe and report on a subculture or societal group. Write a composition in which you explain which anthropological concepts you plan to consider in your report. Make your explanations clear enough for a university student unfamiliar with anthropology to understand. The subculture you are preparing to observe is that of fraternities and/or sororities. Make reference to the Harris (1995) chapter as you explain the concepts that you choose.

```
       Observing Fraternities in Anthropological Views
                          by Kim

     Subculture is the division of large society such
     as this university, which are divided into several
     subgroups according to race, religion, and interst.
     An example of such subgroup is Fraternities at our
     university. Several anthropological concepts can be
     employed in the observation of our fraternities.
        According to Harris, enculturaltion is when the
     old custorms are repeated in the new generation.
     Fraternities at our university clearly demonsrates
     this idea because they pass their values and ideas of
     the group to new initiating brothers from one genera-
     tion to the next. Also, the principles of the organi-
     zation are pressured to the younger brothers by the
     older brothers. For example, the idea that drinking
```

and partying are very acceptable to the group. In addition, they tend to encourage those who party and drink a lot while they discourage those who study and unsocialize. The reason behind this kind of attitude is that drinking and partying are masculine while studying and unsocializing are not.

Another anthropological concept is ethnocentrism. The definition of ethnocentrism according to Harris is the absolute belief that one's own behavior is "normal" while others are "abnormal." Fraternities are an excellent example of this. They see themselves as they are kings and princes of the university. They often display behaviors that are not acceptable to society, yet they do not see it that way. For example, especially when they are walking in a large group, they often behave wildly like yelling and screaming as if they own the campus and others don't exist.

Finally, there are mental and behavioral aspects of culture which can be applied to the Fraternities. The definition of mental and behavioral aspects of culture is that mental concerns with the rules of the society and behavioral concerns with the actual behaviors of the rules. The society has many sanctions against those who break laws such as "no drinking and driving", "no drugs", and "no loud noise after 10 p.m.." Many times in Fraternities, such rules as above are contradicting with their behaviors. For instance, eventhough they know the rule "don't drink and drive," they usually go for a drive after heavy drinking at the party anyway. Another example related to the partying is the rule "do not disturb your neighbor after 10 p.m." They usually end the party around 2 A.M. in the morning!

Overall, several useful anthropological concpets can be employed in the observation of our university Fraternities such as encultration where the cultural traits are passed on from one generation to the next, enthnocentrism where one perceives one's behaviors are normal and perfect while others are abnormal and imperfect, and mental and behavioral aspects where the rules of the society are not correlated with behaviors of human beings.

Anthropology is the study of humankind. And anothropology is also to learn how tranditional human of ancient culture devolop about culture change or stay the same.

What is culture main? It is to learn life style and the way of people's thinking, feeling, and acting. How they change from ancient culture to modern culture, according to the article of "Anthropology and the study of culture" states = Today, nowhere in the world are there elders who know what the children know, no matter how remote and simple the societies are in which the children live. In the past there were always some elders who know more than any children in terms of their experience of having grown up within a culture system. From the article it tells, us, elderly people who doesn't rearly know about young people's thinking. This is culture change. For example, ancient people can not figure-out how moder people fly to the moon. And now we doesn't know how it going to happen on the future after 3th war.

Now culture change to modern. But still have lots off people like to keep some of the tranditional way. For example, from college that have two groups call fraternities and sororities. Fraternities is for male and sororities is for female. These two groups main's to pass tranditional man and women. Furthrmor, if man likes to domainte to women; therefore, they would like to join the fraternities. Because, tranditional man always like to demonite to woman. In addition, if woman thinks home is the only place for woman's "employment". Plus they don't want to work at outside of the world and struggle for their life as men do. Then, they will join in the sororities.

In conclusion, culture change or stay the same, have good point and bad point. Good point is to improve society getting more modern and more convion for people. Bad point is getting more crime happen to

the society. From the article tells us the study of
anthropology remain valuable not so much for the
opportunities. Therefore, goverment should provides
good opportunities for anthropologists to make a good
living, and let them feel comfortable to be anthropologists. Because, people can not work for nothing, they
need make money for living. If government give enough
supporting, than the researcher can do better job to
help the society not getting worth.

---

1 *Imagine you are Kim and June's writing teacher. Respond to the content, rhetoric, and organization of each paper.*

---

2 *Now look again at Kim's and June's papers. This time respond to surface-level language issues (grammar, spelling, punctuation, capitalization, etc.).*

---

3 *How did you record your responses for Kim and June in tasks 1 and 2? by pen? audiotape? computer? This time respond to each paper using another means. Compare and contrast your comments according to the means of response.*

---

4 *In chapter 2 you also met Celia. In her high school ESL class she worked on the series of activities about culture and anthropologists' perspectives described in Chapter 3, pp. 28-29 (suggested by Hilles and Lynch, 1997). As a writing assignment, Celia took on the role of a martian visitor to planet Earth, writing a report home explaining earthlings' eating behaviors. Here is Celia's writing:*

CELIA
ENGLISH CLASS

This is my report to boss at home on my planet Mars.
Poeple on this planet make nurish for thereselves.
On thing they eat called hamburguer. It has bread with
food inside. At first, person pick up hamburguer in
there hands. At second, they put at the mouth and make
big mouthful. At third, they put hamburguer and wipe
mouth with paper. Then they smile because is very good.
I come home to Mars and make hamburguer for everybody.

Imagine you are Celia's writing teacher. Respond to the content, rhetoric, and organization of Celia's writing.

---

5 *Now look again at Celia's writing, this time responding to surface-level language issues (grammar, spelling, punctuation, capitalization, etc.).*

---

6 *How did you record your responses for Celia? by pen? audiotape? computer? This time respond to her writing using another means. Compare and contrast your comments according to the means of response.*

Suggested Readings

Nancie Atwell's (1987) Chapter 5, Lucy Calkins's (1994) Chapter 10, and the Goldstein and Conrad (1990) article are the three most important suggestions I have for more advice from the field about conferring with students about their writing and writing processes. Donald Murray (1984) uses his perceptive teacher's voice to tell a reflective story on conferencing.

For practical ideas about responding on paper to students' writing, take a look at Brinton, Sasser and Winningham (1988), Hendrickson (1984), Leki (1990), and Sommers (1984). While you're at it, you might want to peruse the anthologies the articles appear in.

Those of you who are interested in classroom research on teacher feedback and student response to that feedback should watch for articles by Ferris, Hedgcock, and Lefkowitz, or any combination of the three. For example, Ferris (1995), Ferris (1997), and Hedgcock and Lefkowitz (1994), are all pertinent.

8

Responding to the Writer and His or Her Overall Progress

I was walking down the hall at school, and through an open door I overheard a writing instructor say to his student, "No, not how your *paper* is. How are *you*?" Why is that an unexpected question on a college campus? My colleague continued with his student about the student's bad day and how that had affected the student's time and energy for the paper, and finally decided to reschedule the appointment. Experience in the classroom teaches us that to reach the learner or writer so as to affect his or her work or process, we need to address the person.

Throughout the term I talk to each student about him- or herself as a writer. ("What I really like about the beginning of your paper is the way you. . ." or "Yes, that's a very useful strategy you're using. Many writers do that, and it seems to help them out in these ways. . . ") Most of my students have never conceived of themselves as writers of English. I also get my students to do a lot of reflecting throughout the term on what they're learning and trying out in their writing processes. For the last couple of weeks of the term I compliment each student on writing he or she has been working on. On one of the last days of the term I have my students reread writing they did at the beginning of the term to analyze their own progress in their written work:

> ### SELF-EVALUATION OF SEMESTER PROGRESS
>
> Take a look at the attached sample of your writing from a while ago.
> Think about what we've worked on this semester to improve your writing: making claims and supporting them with evidence, writing complexly with lots of layers of support, making a unifying thesis, making paragraphs and sentences flow smoothly, making good introductions and strong conclusions,

distinguishing between your ideas and those of other
authors, using footnotes and bibliographies, writing
distinctive titles, etc.

Write a brief analysis of how your writing has
improved in our course based on a comparison of
your previous writing with what you can write now.

Amy Tickle has her students do this type of analysis of their writing based on many pieces of writing composed throughout the term. She develops worksheets each time, for each writing assignment, focusing on different rhetorical and process issues. For papers early in the term, Amy might have her students complete worksheets focusing on paragraph unity or cohesiveness or introductions and conclusions. By the end of the term, Amy is confident that each student has plenty of information collected through self-evaluation to write a data-based assessment of his or her own writing. The following are a couple of Amy's worksheets to help students analyze their own writing:

SUMMARY

Directions: Answer the following questions
about your summary.

1. Does my summary mention the source?
Is the source cited correctly?

2. Write the main points covered in your summary.
Are there any other important points that you
need to mention?

3. Is there anything about the summary that
you should take out because it is not an
important main idea?

4. Are there any places in the summary where
you have used editorial comments?

5. Are there any places in the summary
where you have used the original text without
quotation marks?

6. Do you periodically mention the author of
the article throughout the summary?
How many times?

RESEARCH PAPER

DIRECTIONS: Answer the following questions about your paper based on the writing techniques we've learned about in class.

I. GENERAL

1. What is my purpose/main point?

2. Who is my audience?

II. INTRODUCTION

1. What device am I using to begin my paper? For example, asking a question, giving background, using a quotation, etc.

2. Have I included a thesis statement? Write that statement below.

III. BODY

1. What are the main points I am using to support my purpose? List them in an outline form. Are they all related to my purpose?

2. How am I supporting these points? Is the support relevant? Is it enough?

3. Is there any place I need to add citations in my paper because the ideas are not mine nor are they generally known to the public?

4. Does my paper use the proper in-text citations?

5. Have I used too many direct quotations so that it no longer is my paper?

In order to direct her students to evaluate the grammatical structures, spelling, and other issues of form in their own writing, Amy asks them to complete editing checklists that are turned in with each draft. As Amy puts it, by the end of the term the students have well-developed lists of their own frequent mistakes and have, she hopes, improved on their editing skills for these problems.

> As far as encouragement for them to continue to improve in their writing, I think the whole idea of drafting and revising is a tool that nonnative speakers are not really familiar with. Teaching them how to revise a paper is a tool that they will carry with them forever. I encourage *any* revisions a writer makes, even if they're not always effective. (Amy Tickle)

Amy reminisces about a writing mentor in graduate school:

> One thing she told me had a tremendous impact on my writing, and that was to "just say it." Too often writers are so concerned with "how" they say something, they get frustrated. And often, especially ESL writers, the writers end up writing something that doesn't make sense because they are trying to package the idea in sophisticated wording. So I always encourage my students to try writing without any pressure of how something is said. In the end, I hope they see writing as something other than a horrific burden. Journals are a good tool for this. I also tell my students that writing is like exercise—the more you do it, the easier it gets and the better you become.

Portfolios are used often as a demonstration of long-term writing progress, both in individual writing classes and in whole programs. At Berkeley Melinda Erickson (Chapter 3) and her colleagues require all freshman composition students to produce a portfolio of work drawn from writing they have done during the term. In order to successfully complete the freshman composition requirement, the students need to achieve passing marks on coursework graded by their own teachers throughout the term, as well as on the portfolio graded by their teacher and another faculty member at the end of the term. For the portfolio the students compile a number of pieces of their writing from the course in order to demonstrate a good command of a variety of types of academic writing along with drafts that brought their work to completion. As Melinda describes the portfolio process, the students engage in a great deal of self-evaluation. They assess the strengths and weaknesses of their work across the term, as well as evaluate how pieces of their writing fit together to form pictures of themselves as writers. After selecting the pieces for the portfolio, each student writes an introduction explaining the context of each piece and why it was included. The self-evaluation needed on the part of the students to compose this introduction can lead, as Melinda points out, to closer reading of earlier writing, which, in turn, may lead to further revisions.

Much of the impact of the portfolio is the neat and orderly presentation of a large quantity of writing: "Wow! I wrote all that! It's beautiful!" as my student, Keiko, exclaimed last fall. It's the thrill of publication! Melinda's students also get published in a class volume. Melinda facilitates this by having her students bring a class set of copies of one paper they wrote that semester, recollating them, and adding a table of contents and a cover sheet. "As informal as this is, I'm always surprised at how students seem to like to see their names in the table of contents and how they begin to read through the collection right on the spot," reports Melinda. Likewise, Ron Balsamo, the creative writing teacher from Chapter 4, uses essays from his former students as examples in an informally assembled "textbook" for his writing class. The textbook's overall exposition remains the same, but Ron alternates sample essays. As he says, "When I ask students during the course if I may use their essay for the next book, they simply go wild. When they learn that their essay actually made it into the volume, they run to the bookstore for a copy or copies even though they're no longer in the course. Students in the course often know the students whose essays appear in the text, which seems to appeal to them and which inspires them as they see what others like them have been able to do."

After all the blood, sweat, and tears, we see language develop and our students emerge as writers. For years I've thought of portfolios as giving us a view of our writing students' progress across time. In some cases they do. The portfolio system used in Melinda's program at Berkeley is similar to other portfolio systems I am familiar with. (Each student selects representative pieces of writing he or she has done throughout the term or program, improves them, and introduces them in a self-evaluative opening essay to be submitted along with the representative pieces and sometimes with earlier drafts.) In order to see progress the student has made across time the pieces need to be selected according to that criterion and the self-evaluation needs to address developmental progress. On the other hand, the student may choose to leave all of that to implication in order to focus more overtly on his or her identity as a writer. In collaborating with me for this book, Melinda made me realize that the portfolio, instead of fundamentally providing an indication of the writer's progress, might actually give us something closer to a proficiency measure; a highly contextualized, broad measure of writing proficiency. In any case, portfolios clearly give instructors far more information about students and their writing than other means of writing assessment. I, for one, am grateful that the portfolio has replaced the timed essay in many academic situations requiring writing assessment.

One of the most important aspects of portfolio processes (regardless of the procedural details) is the natural way the student evaluates his or her own work. Self-evaluation takes place when the student selects the individual pieces of writing to include in the portfolio, during any further revision that may take place, and often analytically in writing as a component of the portfolio. Students need training in carrying out this type of self-evaluation. The worksheets Amy uses to direct her students to evaluate their own essays provide the type of practice reflection that can, by the end of a term, grow into a thorough self-evaluation of a body of work. Whether or not portfolios are used at your school, it is important to develop in your students an ability to evaluate writing quality and a critical awareness of ways to strengthen their own writing.

Compliments on a turn of phrase and advice on how to continue improving writing after the course ends offer a certain friendly encouragement. But putting a student's name in print, publishing the student's work—even informally—goes far toward making that student a writer of English for life.

---

1 *Brainstorm various ways, other than adding up individual grades at the end of the term, to arrive at an overall course grade, to evaluate the long-term progress students have made on their writing throughout a school term. In what teaching situations does each make sense?*

2 *What are reasons (or teaching situations) for grading written products versus the writing process, and vice versa?*

3 *Think of a specific type of writing course for a specific group of students. Design prompts that will encourage self-evaluation on the part of the students, both during your course and after it has ended.*

4 *What types of writing (i.e., sample portfolio contents) might be collected in student portfolios for the following:*

a. EFL university preparation courses at a private school

b. ESL at an adult school/community college, intermediate level

c. ESL in a secondary school, college preparatory track, intermediate level

d. ESL pull-out class in a middle school

5 *Given the student portfolios in each of the four cases in # 4, what criteria will you use to evaluate the portfolios? Compare and contrast them.*

Suggested Readings

For more teacher voices and classroom-based discussion of writing assessment, see Chapter 12 of Kathleen Bailey's (1998) volume, *Learning about Language Assessment: Dilemmas, Decisions, and Directions.*

Pick up whatever you see by Liz Hamp-Lyons for insight into assessing ESL students' writing progress. A good place to start is her (1996) article.

Still the best anthology on portfolio assesssment is *Portfolios: Process and Product*, edited by Belanoff and Dickson (1991).

9

REFLECTING ON YOUR PEDAGOGICAL PLANS FOR TEACHING WRITING

If writing processes vary like pinball games, then what can we learn about teaching writing from teaching pinball? Teaching pinball must be like teaching horseback riding, photography, or scuba diving: the teacher can talk a blue streak and give demonstrations left, right, and center, but the learning really begins when the teacher hands over the responsibility to the students and stands back to watch, offering encouragement and advice. From the act of writing and being made aware of (and trying out) a variety of writing strategies for different purposes, students eventually develop a sense of authority over their writing, even in another language.

Much of what I have described in this book may appear demanding for ESL students in middle and high schools. In my opinion, bringing more challenge into public schools is exactly what is needed. Not long ago I came across a comment from a recent high school graduate, reported by Brinton and Mano (1994). I had read it before, but this time it hit home.

> The ESL classes in our schools don't have a challenging curriculum, most of it. . . It's. . . giving you. . . books that have the big print and stuff like that for you to read. . . it had a bad connotation in high school. (Brinton and Mano, 1994, p. 15)

It is every teacher's responsibility to engage students and push them to think about the world in new and exciting ways. Books with big print or lots of decontextualized exercises don't seem very interesting to you or me—why expect our students to be motivated by them? Listen to your students to find out what does hook them, and then guide them in ways to look at things from different perspectives. That's the basis of critical thinking, and what better place to work on developing critical thinking than in an ESL writing class?

Back in Chapter One I explained what I had experienced as a writing student in my native language and how I believe this history relates to my writing principles and pedagogy. At this point in my career as a writing instructor, I now have my own substantial history of teaching to also relate to my pedagogical beliefs. The spin I now bring to my teaching of writing is that what I am really teaching students to do is work with text. "Teaching writing" is a misnomer for what I do, just as "teaching grammar" is a misnomer for what any communicative language instructor does. Yes, our jobs sometimes entail isolating *writing* from the larger notion of *text* and isolating *grammar* from *communication*; but the point is, we are teaching rich, useful, live communication practices complete with accompanying social expectations and surrounding culture. As communicative language teachers we teach worlds more—literally—than the four skills, which remain dissected components of language. As a "writing" teacher I choose to teach students ways to admire, imagine, appraise, and fabricate text while they write and read. Along the way, I also teach critical thinking and creativity and offer opportunities to overcome barriers to text, class, and academia.

Take some time now to reflect on your teaching plans. What are you going to be teaching in your upcoming ESL writing class? Will you follow the historical path of language pedagogy and dissect writing from reading, speaking, listening, and thinking? There is no question that your teaching task will become far simpler than if you attempt what I am suggesting here. For one thing, there are plenty of writing textbooks on the market that provide straightforward, simple (but unfortunately reductive and simplified) course structures for you to follow. But if you choose a path like those taken by teachers KimMarie, Melinda, Ron, Rona, Amy, and myself, you will build elaborately on the notion of writing, integrating reading, imagination, self-exploration, and technology into your course in expansive and exciting ways. Instead of thinking of your students as a class, you will visualize each individual face, personality, background, and voice. You will watch each of your students closely, guiding them in ways to experiment with text and thereby learn about language and life. Your teaching job will become harder, but it will also be far more challenging, as will the ideas and text your second-language students create. The challenge will bring you and your students rich satisfaction.

Teaching writing is not an easy task; nor is writing itself. As your teaching process continues, maintain an attitude of inquiry and continue learning from your students.

---

1 *Return to your answers from the "investigations" section in Chapter 1 (pp. 4-5). Now that you've become more aware of issues in the field of teaching ESL writing, reexamine your earlier thoughts. In what ways has your thinking expanded beyond those initial ideas? What can you add to those memories of your past experience as a student of writing that will help you become a more understanding and more critical language instructor?*

---

2 *Go to a nearby library, ESL learning center, or teacher materials room that has recent textbooks for teaching ESL writing. Better yet, go to a local conference at which publishers display their textbooks. Glance over the ESL writing textbooks you find, selecting some that interest you. For each textbook you examine, determine whether the book is a reference handbook, a composition textbook (usually called a "rhetoric"), or a sourcebook of readings for analysis (usually called a "reader"). Take note of the book's general format or major sec-*

tions, especially unusual characteristics. How well does the textbook address issues we've been studying here? Which student groups in which types of courses would most benefit from the book?

3 Contact the nearest office of the National Writing Project (look for them on the Internet) for information about upcoming workshops or conferences. Plan to attend an event soon with classmates or colleagues.

4 Imagine that you are applying for one of the following jobs.

In this ESL writing position you would be teaching first-year college composition courses to both foreign students newly arrived in this country and immigrant students who have lived in English-speaking countries and attended public schools using English for several years.

In this ESL writing position you would be teaching English writing to adults in Saturday classes at a private school. The students are mostly laborers and professionals; most of them work full-time, with a few students working part-time.

In this ESL position you will be teaching secondary-school students in a large urban area. Most of the students are Asian and Hispanic. Except for daily ESL, these students are mainstreamed in courses with native speakers of English.

In this ESL position you will be teaching Spanish-speaking middle-school students who are pulled out of social studies class each day in order to receive ESL writing instruction.

Brainstorm your answers to the following interview questions:

a. How would you approach this teaching situation? What would your course generally look like? What kinds of materials would you use? What textbooks would be appropriate?

b. What kinds of activities would you do in your class to get students to improve their strategies for getting started? for revising? for proofreading?

c. How do you approach giving feedback on their writing to students?

d. Some of the writing teachers in our department spend lots of time conferencing individually with students. Whenever I walk down the hall I see these teachers at their desks, poring over papers with individual students. Frankly, I think it is more efficient to teach the class as a whole. How do *you* feel about conferencing?

e. What do you know about the portfolio system of assessment? How might this work as an exit procedure for students completing our program? Would you ever use portfolios in an individual class you might teach?

f. What is one influential principle (or set of principles) that encompasses your approach to teaching writing?

g. Why do you want to become a writing teacher?

Glossary

Applied linguistics: An academic discipline relating linguistics to other areas of study, e.g., language acquisition, education, psychology, and sociology, particularly in order to better understand the teaching and learning of languages.

Appropriating language: Taking over the language of another person or group for one's own use, intentions, or purposes. Refers, for example, to what a writing teacher does when mistakenly assuming a student writer intends certain ideas in an early draft and accordingly giving the student advice for "improving" the draft, advice which may not fit with the student's plans.

Audience: The group or person, however abstract, to whom a writer intends to communicate meaning through his or her written text.

Audiolingual language pedagogy: A language teaching method used predominantly in the U.S. during the 1950's and 1960's, based on the notions that listening to and repeating dialogues and structural components of a language must occur before reading and writing, and that language learning is a matter of habit formation.

Authentic text: Written text used in language study, text which was originally produced for purposes other than language learning (e.g., subject matter textbook excerpts, poetry, autobiographies, Internet information, newspaper passages).

Authenticity: An important notion in communicative language teaching, the extent to which materials and tasks used for language teaching and learning represent naturally-occurring, purposeful (vs. simplified, decontextualized) text, speech, and activities.

Authority: Control over language and language use, particularly regarding a person's understanding, and confidence in that understanding, of reading text or writing strategies.

Autonomy: A quality enabling a person to interact with text or accomplish some other language task in a self-directed manner without significant or constant assistance from others.

Background sources: Text or other materials used as information for developing ideas or as support for a writer's claims made in writing or formal speaking.

Brainstorming: A technique for generating a pool of ideas in order to eventually select the most appropriate ideas for use in writing or some other creative task.

Breadth course or breadth requirement: In higher education, especially in the U.S., a course focusing on subject matter that is outside the core or major area of study, but supplementary to it. Sometimes taking this type of course, which offers breadth to the student's education, is required for graduation.

Chain stories: A comprehension-production teaching technique involving students in creating short segments of a story and passing the whole emerging story on to another student in class; that next student needs to continue the story according to everything that has been produced thus far, before passing everything on to another student in class who will continue the production of the story by adding another segment.

Citation: A reference to another author or written source, especially relevant to academic writing which obliges the writer to acknowledge authors of other sources that are summarized, paraphrased, or quoted. The typical form of citation in academic writing includes three components: a phrase like "according to. . ." or "As. . . indicates. . ." along with a footnote and a bibliographical entry.

Clustering: A technique for helping students generate ideas for writing and begin to organize those ideas. Learners are encouraged to think of as many ideas as possible that are relevant to a writing assignment, and thereafter to draw lines circling (or clustering) the ideas that seem to most closely relate to each other. Sometimes helpful for visual learners who can draw in connections that they did not perceive from purely verbal speech or text. See also mapping.

Collaborative learning: A means of study where learners work together, sharing their knowledge and resources to produce better learning outcomes, for example, better written essays, than if they worked in isolation without the input of their peers.

Critical thinking: Instead of referring to a negative frame of mind, this notion relates to the type of reasoning that involves evaluation, critique, and the juxtaposition of values, standards, or attitudes.

Critical literacy: An educational philosophy that expands the notion of an ability to read and write (literacy) to include an understanding of society and ways to take action to improve one's place in society.

Conferencing: A means of offering student writers feedback during the writing process, where the teacher meets (usually individually) with a student writer to discuss revision options on a draft, the strategies the student is using to write and revise the work, and the student's progress as a writer.

Content: A notion referring to the ideas or subject matter that provide the substance that people read and/or write about, as opposed to linguistic or rhetorical features of text.

Content-based writing courses: Courses in which writing instruction emerges from ideas or subject matter that hold the primary focus of the curriculum, e.g., revolving themes centered around social issues, or academic subjects such as history, anthropology, or political science. Students read, analyze, and draw from authentic text of the content area as a means of learning about the content while also learning about writing.

Content courses: Courses focusing primarily on subject matter (e.g., history, anthropology, chemistry) rather than on writing or other areas of language use.

Context: The linguistic or social environment in which language components (e.g., words, phrases, paragraphs, essays, conversations) are used, especially important in determining meaning and purpose of the language.

Contextualization: The notion of putting language into a meaningful environment, situation, or context, in order to make it easier to learn or understand. In this case, language might refer to words, phrases, paragraphs, essays, conversations, writing tasks, class activities, teacher explanations, etc.

Cubing: A technique for generating ideas for writing where writers quickly take notes on six different aspects of a subject, (1) describing it, (2) comparing it, (3) associating it, (4) analyzing it, (5) applying it, and (6) arguing for or against it.

Dialogical thinking: A thinking process that writers follow who move back and forth in a dialogue-like way between furthering their writing (producing and editing words, phrases, and sentences) and backtracking to reread, reconsider and digest what they've written or what their assignment calls for.

Diction: Corresponding to its meaning regarding clear pronunciation, this term is used in composition to refer to word choice and how appropriate and effective the choice of wording is in various types of writing.

Discourse units: Segments of language beyond the sentence level, e.g., paragraphs, introductions, conclusions, summaries, critiques, poems, essays, interviews, conversations.

EAP: The abbreviation for English for academic purposes. See that entry below.

Editing: Making corrections and improvements to words, grammar, spelling, punctuation, and capitalization in writing. In contrast, see revision.

Editing checklists: Lists that students use to keep track of grammar points, spelling problems, and other editing issues that they need to remember to improve in drafts of their writing.

E-mail: The abbreviation for electronic mail. See that entry below.

Electronic mail: Messages that can be sent electronically from one computer to another by way of the Internet.

Enculturation: An anthropological term referring to the way people of a culture pass on their values, beliefs, and traditions to following generations.

English for academic purposes: A pedagogical approach concerned with teaching those aspects of the English language needed for successful study in higher education for students immersed in an English-speaking college or university setting (notetaking from lectures and textbooks, summarizing, writing term papers, doing library research, etc.).

Ethnocentrism: A term from anthropology referring to the attitude that one's own culture or societal group is superior to others'.

Expository writing: Writing typically used in academic settings, involving the explanation and discussion of information in order to clarify and make the information understandable. As a rhetorical mode, expository writing is an umbrella-term covering definition, comparison, contrast, classification, analogy, cause and effect, analysis, and illustration.

Extrinsic motivation: A drive or desire to perform well based on some sort of outside reward or reason beyond the self (e.g., writing polished prose for good grades, or for praise from others, or to get into college, or to get a job, etc.). In contrast, see intrinsic motivation.

Feedback: Response that indicates the extent to which information is understandable; regarding writing, the response of a teacher, mentor, peer, or some other outside reader to a writer's work, particularly as such response helps facilitate improved writing.

Five-paragraph composition structure: A simple essay organization involving one paragraph of introduction, followed by three paragraphs within the body of the essay, and ending with one paragraph of conclusion.

Five-paragraph essay: A simple composition made up of one paragraph of introduction, followed by three paragraphs within the body of the essay, and ending with one paragraph of conclusion.

Freewriting: A technique to encourage fluency or to generate ideas to be honed later for more concise, organized composition.

General education course or general education requirement: In higher education, especially in the U.S., a course focusing on general subject matter which is outside the specific core or major area of study, but supplementary to it. Sometimes taking this type of course is required for graduation. See breadth course, above.

Global errors: From error analysis, this term refers to errors in major components of the structure of a sentence (e.g., the interaction among tense, aspect, and adverbials in verb phrases or placement of relative clauses), errors that usually cause misunderstanding. In contrast, see local errors.

Grade-point average: A numerical calculation representing the overall average of course grades for individual students in U.S. secondary schools, colleges, and universities, with 4.0 being maximum.

Heuristics: Learning processes for generating ideas and discovering on one's own accord procedures for further inquiry. In writing, this term is used to refer to techniques like listing, clustering, mapping, brainstorming, freewriting—whatever writers do at the very beginning of their writing processes to get their ideas flowing.

Homepage: The first page, or top-level document, in an electronic site on the World-Wide Web; in other words, the first page of information seen by someone accessing the site through the Web, from which the person might connect to other pages or other sites through built-in links. Many corporations, universities, businesses, and individuals have their own homepage to make themselves accessible on the World-Wide Web.

In-class essays: Compositions written in class, usually to practice timed writing (see below) as is sometimes required for essay examinations in secondary schools, colleges, and universities, as well as for some standardized examinations.

Inner dialogue: An unspoken dialogue occurring as part of a thinking process that writers follow who move back and forth between furthering their writing (producing and editing words, phrases, and sentences) and backtracking to reread, reconsider and digest what they've written or what their assignment calls for.

Integrated-skills course: A language course that integrates writing, reading, speaking, and listening practice.

Interacting with text: Actively contemplating or manipulating written text through reading, writing, and critical thinking.

Internet: A world-wide electronic network interconnecting computer systems such that communication can occur between computers nearly instantaneously.

Intrinsic motivation: An inner drive or desire to perform well for no other apparent reason except that the activity itself is rewarding (e.g., writing polished prose for the sense of accomplishment or because the challenge is self-satisfying). In contrast, see extrinsic motivation.

Jigsaw reading: A means of collaborative learning where related readings are divided up among students, each of whom studies his or her own particular reading, preparing to discuss it, in order to inform the others in class; together the whole class discusses, compares, and synthesizes issues in the readings, putting the jigsaw pieces together for an understanding of the whole.

Journals: Besides referring to academic periodicals, this term is used for diary-like reflective notebooks that students maintain for regular writing practice, sometimes involving regular feedback from the teacher (called dialogue journals) or documenting responses to reading assignments (also called reading journals, reading logs, or learning logs).

Learning processes: What learners go through as their understanding of knowledge unfolds, ideally involving the conscious use of learning strategies for making the formation of the understanding take place efficiently.

Linear writing process: The course of action taken when a person follows one step after another in order to develop a piece of writing, where each step needs to be completed before moving on to the next step; or when a writer composes one sentence after another, such that each sentence needs to be correct before the writer moves on to the following sentence. In contrast, see recursive writing process.

Listing: A technique for helping students generate ideas for writing. Learners are encouraged to make a long list of as many ideas as they can possibly think of that relate to the writing assignment.

Local errors: From error analysis, this term refers to errors in minor syntactic components of a sentence (e.g., the articles *a*, *an*, or *the*), errors that do not often affect the overall meaning of the sentence. In contrast, see global errors.

Mainstream content courses: Courses in U.S. elementary and secondary schools that are not ESL related, which native speakers of English take and which non-native speakers of English take if their English language proficiency allows them to be successful. These include courses such as social studies, science, mathematics, music, and art.

Mapping: A technique for generating ideas to be used in writing and for beginning to organize those ideas. The writer jots words and phrases down on paper in a haphazard order, and then begins drawing lines, like roads or pathways, to connect related ideas while continuing to add new ideas. Sometimes helpful for visual learners who can draw in connections that they did not perceive from purely verbal speech or text. Sometimes called semantic mapping.

Means of response: In teaching writing, this refers to the way in which the writing teacher gives the student feedback on a written draft or final paper, e.g., by writing in the margin of the paper; by recording comments on audiotape; by typing comments into a computer file, sometimes using an editing program; or by conferencing in person with the student.

Mental and behavioral aspects of culture: Anthropological terms used to refer to perceptions of one's culture versus actual examples of conduct by people in one's culture.

Mini-assignments: Rather than complete essays or papers, this term refers to short assignments done in a writing course to help the students practice a particular aspect of writing, e.g., defining terms or summarizing.

Multiskills course: A language course that offers students practice in writing, reading, speaking, and listening.

Negotiation of meaning: A notion referring to the what speakers do in naturally- occurring conversation to make each other understood; for example, during a conference with a teacher and a student discussing the student's draft of a writing assignment, this refers to the talk between both speakers that takes place in order to clarify the student's intentions and meaning in his/her writing.

Organization: In written text, the structure of paragraphs, essays, and longer stretches of discourse, i.e., the structure beyond the sentence level in written discourse.

Paraphrasing: Using different phrasing and wording (requiring citation) to express a particular passage that was originally written or spoken by someone else, in order to blend the other's idea smoothly into one's own writing.

Peer review: Learners giving each other feedback on writing-in-progress in order to encourage revision.

Portfolios: Collections of writing that provide a variety of samples of the writer's work produced for different assignments and purposes, used in assessment of student writing across time, including self-reflection by the student on the body of work.

Premature editing: A notion referring to the way some writers work a great amount of time on each phrase and sentence they write in order to get every detail of grammar, wording, and spelling correct before moving on to the next sentence; some outcomes of premature editing are that the writers usually find it difficult to keep an overall plan of ideas in mind and that they may have trouble producing text of much length.

Prewriting: Activities that take place in preparation of actual drafting of text, e.g., heuristics, taking notes on library or Internet research.

Process-oriented pedagogy: An approach to teaching writing that involves the teacher and student in working on strategies for analyzing text, generating ideas, pre-writing, drafting, revising, redrafting, proofreading, and other activities that occur during the process of writing. See writing processes below.

Process writing: What a writer engages in who consciously strategizes and undertakes ways to generate ideas and produce pre-writing, to draft and redraft, to revise, to evaluate his or her own writing, to proofread, and other activities important for producing good writing.

Product-oriented pedagogy: An approach to teaching writing that involves the analysis of sample readings and repeated production of single drafts of writing.

Proofreading: Making corrections and improvements to words, grammar, spelling, punctuation, and capitalization in writing. In contrast, see revision.

Proofreading checklists: Lists that students use to keep track of grammar points, spelling problems and other editing issues that they need to remember to improve in drafts of their writing.

Purpose: A reason behind one's writing that is particularly meaningful to the individual writer and that determines that writer's approach to the assignment or writing task, i.e., something that an individual writer wants to accomplish, given an assignment or writing task; something that will distinguish that writer's work from another's.

Reader-based prose: Written text that includes enough explanation, context, and organizational cues for the reader to easily understand the writer's purpose and meaning; such text smoothly communicates the writer's intent to the reader. In contrast, see writer-based prose.

Readers: Textbooks used in composition courses with sample essays, articles, and sometimes poetry, usually organized around themes or rhetorical modes; such textbooks include questions for prompting class discussions and writing projects. This term also refers to writing specialists who read and evaluate diagnostic writing exams, portfolios, and standardized essay exams.

Recursive writing process: The course of action taken when a person drafts writing and continuously returns to an earlier section to revise briefly before moving ahead with where the person left off; or when a writer composes, and repeatedly returns to previous spots for a quick revision before continuing with the writing. In contrast, see linear writing process.

Revision: Changes that a writer makes to a draft in progress, changes that affect meaning, organization, the writer's approach to the topic or task, etc. Such changes might include adding sentences or paragraphs, moving sentences or paragraphs around and adding appropriate transitions, alternating repeated terms with synonyms, throwing out a concluding paragraph and rewriting it altogether, etc. In contrast, see proofreading or editing.

Rhetoric: In the field of writing, this notion most often refers to approaches to writing based on classical tradition (4th century B.C.) involving the analysis of audience, invention, persuasive techniques to formulate arguments, the arrangement or organization of ideas, style, etc.

Rhetorics: Textbooks used in composition courses which focus primarily on explanations of ways to prepare, organize, and polish good writing. Such textbooks are often organized around rhetorical modes.

Rhetorical modes: Types of written products based on their approach and organization: exposition (definition, comparison, contrast, classification, analogy, cause and effect, analysis, exemplification, and illustration), description, narration, and persuasion.

Rhetorical strategy: The deliberate use of rhetorical structure to accomplish specific intention or purpose in writing.

Rhetorical structure: The line of reasoning of a written product in terms of its approach and the rhetorical modes (narration, persuasion, etc.) used throughout.

Scanning: In reading, moving your line of vision swiftly across and down a page of text in order to locate specific bits of information quickly.

Sentence-level language issues: Language components of a sentence, e.g., grammar, word usage, spelling, punctuation, capitalization, etc.

Skimming: In reading, moving your line of vision swiftly across and down a page of text in order to grasp the main idea, while ignoring details.

Summarizing: Using different, more general, and fewer words (requiring citation) to express information, sometimes merely the main idea or a part of some information originally written or spoken by someone else, in order to blend the other's ideas smoothly into one's own writing.

Thesis: In the organization of an essay, the thesis is a statement of one or two sentences that clarifies the overall topic and purpose of the entire essay.

Timed writing: Compositions written under time pressure in class, usually to practice writing for essay examinations as is sometimes required in secondary schools, colleges, and universities, as well as for some standardized examinations.

Topic-based guidelines: A set of prompts for encouraging students to improve the ideas presented in their writing, prompts based on the particular topic of the given assignment, as opposed to guidelines based on rhetorical approach or generic essay structure.

Topic-based worksheet: Like topic-based guidelines, a topic-based worksheet presents students with a set of activities to further develop ideas presented in their writing, activities based on the particular topic of the given assignment, as opposed to rhetorical approach or generic essay structure. Used often in content-based teaching.

Topic sentence: In the organization of an essay, a topic sentence is that sentence in each paragraph of the body of the essay that clarifies the main idea of its paragraph.

Travel literature: Essays and memoirs written about observations, adventures, and transitions a writer has experienced in various communities and cultures. Highly reflective of one's self, one's own culture, and foreign communities and cultures.

Travel writing: Besides being a synonym for travel literature, this refers to the act of producing such written work, i.e., a type of writing you might have your second-language students create.

Uniform resource locators: Addresses used on the World-Wide Web for locating information on the Internet.

URLs: The abbreviation for uniform resource locators. See that entry above.

World-Wide Web: A system for accessing online resources on the Internet.

Writer-based prose: Written text that expresses the writer's thoughts in ways that do not communicate completely to an outside reader; such text may appear unfocused, underdeveloped, lacking context, including tangential information, and other problems. In other words, the writer understands his or her text, but it has not been shaped in ways to communicate the meaning and intent to a reader. In contrast, see reader-based prose.

Writing across the curriculum: A movement promoting the concern for and use of implicit, if not explicit, instruction in excellence in writing among instructional faculty in all academic disciplines, as opposed to leaving writing instruction to the writing teachers.

Writing from sources: Using information from background sources or previous research to support claims being made in new written text.

Writing processes: The sequences of activities that writers go through when producing text, activities like compiling information, generating ideas, drafting, revising, redrafting, proofreading, etc. Such sequences vary according to the writing task, the writer's experience with that task, pressure on the writer to finish quickly or produce polished work, etc.

Writing task: Any example of written work, from jotting down a phone message for a coworker to writing a review of this book. In writing courses, writing tasks are designed for the student to work toward a particular meaningful objective with the purpose of experiencing and gaining an understanding of writing and writing processes.

Writing workshop: An atmosphere fostering concentration on producing effective written work by individuals, pairs, and small groups of people, with and without teachers or tutors. Important to a writing workshop is the availability of plenty of informational resources (books, articles, the Internet, etc.) and tools for writing (computers, paper, pens, and other office supplies).

Written products: Complete pieces of written text, e.g., essays, poems, e-mail messages, research papers, newspaper columns, or written answers to questions.

References

Atwell, N. 1987. *In the middle: Writing, reading, and learning with adolescents.* Portsmouth, NH: Boynton/Cook.

Belanoff, P,. and M. Dickson (eds.). 1991. *Portfolios: Process and product.* Portsmouth, NH: Boynton/Cook.

Belcher, D., and G. Braine (eds.). 1995. *Academic writing in a second language: Essays on research and pedagogy.* Norwood, NJ: Ablex.

Bradbury, R. 1950. *The martian chronicles.* Garden City, NY: Doubleday.

Bradbury, R. 1990. *Zen in the art of writing.* Santa Barbara, CA: Joshua Odell Editions, Capra Press.

Bridgeman, B., and S. B. Carlson. 1984. Survey of academic writing tasks. *Written Communication* 1: 247–280.

Brinton, D., J. Goodwin, and L. Ranks. 1994. Helping language minority students read and write analytically: The journey into, through, and beyond. In F. Peitzman and G. Gadda (eds.), *With different eyes: Insights into teaching language minority students across the disciplines.* Reading, MA: Addison-Wesley.

Brinton, D., and S. Mano. 1994. "You have a chance also": Case histories of ESL students at the university. In F. Peitzman and G. Gadda (eds.), *With different eyes: Insights into teaching language minority students across the disciplines.* Reading, MA: Addison-Wesley.

Brinton, D., L. Sasser, and B. Winningham. 1988. The limited English proficient student. In G. Gadda, F. Peitzman, and W. Walsh (eds.), *Teaching analytical writing.* Los Angeles: California Academic Partnership Program.

Calkins, L. M. 1994. *The art of teaching writing.* Portsmouth, NH: Heinemann.

Campbell, C. 1987. Writing with others' words: The use of information from a background reading text in the writing of native and nonnative university composition students. Unpublished doctoral dissertation, Program in Applied Linguistics, University of California, Los Angeles.

Campbell, C. 1990. Writing with others' words: Using background reading text in academic compositions. In B. Kroll (ed.), *Second language writing: Research insights for the classroom.* Cambridge, UK: Cambridge University Press.

Carson, J. G., and I. Leki (eds.). 1993. *Reading in the composition classroom: Second language perspectives.* Boston: Heinle & Heinle.

Carson J. G., and G. L. Nelson. 1994. Writing groups: Cross-cultural issues. *Journal of Second Language Writing* 3: 17–30.

Clark, C. L. 1996. *A student's guide to the Internet.* Upper Saddle River, NJ: Prentice-Hall.

Codrescu, A. 1993. *Road scholar: Coast to coast late in the century.* New York: Hyperion.

Connor, U., and R. B. Kaplan (eds.). 1987. *Writing across languages: Analysis of L2 text.* Reading, MA: Addison-Wesley.

Cooper, M. M., and M. Holzman. 1989. *Writing as social action.* Portsmouth, NH: Boynton/Cook.

Crump, E., and N. Carbone. 1997. *English online: A student's guide to the Internet and World Wide Web.* Boston: Houghton Mifflin.

Danish, B. 1981. *Writing as a second language: A workbook for writing and teaching writing.* New York: Teachers and Writers.

DeVillar, R. A., and C. J. Faltis. 1991. *Computers and cultural diversity: Restructuring for school success.* Albany, NY: State University of New York Press.

Early, M., C. Thew, and P. Wakefield. 1986. *Integrating language and content instruction K–12: An ESL resource book.* Victoria, BC, Canada: Publications Service Branch, Ministry of Education.

Elbow, P. 1986. *Writing with Power.* Oxford and New York: Oxford University Press.

Ferris, D. 1995. Student reactions to teacher response in multiple-draft composition studies. *TESOL Quarterly* 29: 33–53.

Ferris, D. 1997. The influence of teacher commentary on student revision. *TESOL Quarterly* 31: 315–339.

Ferris, D., and J. Hedgcock. 1998. *Purpose, process, and practice: Research and theory in teaching ESL composition.* Working title. Mahwah, NJ: Lawrence Erlbaum.

Flower, L. 1984. Writer-based prose: A cognitive basis for problems in writing. In S. McKay (ed.), *Composing in a second language.* Rowley, MA: Newbury House, 16–42. Also appeared in *College English* 41 (1979): 19–37.

Freedman, A., I. Pringle, and J. Yalden (eds.). 1983. *Learning to write: 1st language/2nd language.* New York: Longman.

Fong-Torres, B. 1994. *The rice room: Growing up Chinese-American: From number two son to rock 'n' roll.* New York: Hyperion.

Fu, D. 1995. *"My trouble is my English": Asian students and the American dream.* Portsmouth, NH: Boynton/Cook Publishers.

Gere, A. R. 1987. *Writing groups: History, theory, and implications.* Carbondale: Southern Illinois Press.

Grabe, W., and R. B. Kaplan. 1996. *Theory and practice of writing.* London: Longman.

Goldberg, N. 1986. *Writing down the bones: Freeing the writer within.* Boston: Shambhala Publications.

Goldstein, L., C. Campbell, and M. C. Cummings. 1997. Smiling through the turbulence: The flight attendant syndrome and other issues of writing instructor status in the adjunct model. In M. A. Snow and D. M. Brinton (eds.), *The content-based classroom: Perspectives on integrating language and content.* White Plains, NY: Longman. Also appeared in *CATESOL Journal* 7 (1994): 19–29.

Goldstein, L. M., and S. M. Conrad. 1990. Student input and negotiation of meaning in ESL writing conferences. *TESOL Quarterly* 24: 441–460.

Hafernik, J. J. 1983. The how and why of peer editing in the ESL writing class (ED253064). Washington, DC: ERIC Document Reproduction.

Hairston, M. 1982. The winds of change: Thomas Kuhn and the revolution in the teaching of writing. *College Composition and Communication* 33: 76.

Hale, G., et al. 1996. A study of writing tasks assigned in academic degree programs. *Research Report* 54 (June). Princeton, NJ: Educational Testing Service.

Hamp-Lyons, L. 1996. The challenges of second-language writing assessment. In E. M. White, W. D. Lutz, and S. Kamusikiri (eds.), *Assessment of writing: Politics, policies, practices.* New York: Modern Language Association, 226–240.

Harris, M. 1995. *Cultural anthropology.* New York: Addison-Wesley Educational Books.

Heath, S. B., and L. Mangiola. 1991. *Children of promise: Literature activity in linguistically and culturally diverse classrooms.* Washington, DC: National Education Association.

Hedgcock, J., and N. Lefkowitz. 1994. Feedback on feedback: Assessing learner receptivity to teacher response in L2 composing. *Journal of Second Language Writing* 3: 141–163.

Hendrickson, J. 1984. The treatment of error in written work. In S. McKay (ed.), *Composing in a second language.* Rowley, MA: Newbury House.

Hilles, S., and D. Lynch. 1997. Culture as content. In M. A. Snow and D. M. Brinton (eds.), *The content-based classroom: Perspectives on integrating language and content.* White Plains, NY: Longman.

Hillocks, G. 1995. *Teaching writing as reflective practice.* New York: Teachers College Press.

Hoffman, E. 1989. *Lost in translation: A life in a new language.* New York: Penguin.

Iyer, P. 1988. *Video night in Kathmandu: And other reports from the not-so-far east.* New York: Knopf.

James, D. R. 1981. Peer teaching in the writing classroom. *English Journal* 70: 48–50.

Johnson, D., and D. Roen (eds.). 1989. *Richness in writing: Empowering ESL students.* New York: Longman.

Johnson, K. E. 1998. *Manual for teachers understanding teaching: A multimedia hypertext tool for TeacherSource.* Version 1.01. Boston: Heinle & Heinle.

Kagan, S. 1988. *Cooperative learning resources for teachers.* Laguna Niguel, CA: Resources for Teachers.

Kluckhohn, C. 1949. Mirror for man. Reprinted in J. R. McCuen and A. C. Winkler (eds.), *Readings for Writers* (4th ed.). New York: Harcourt Brace Jovanovich, 226–233.

Kroll, B. (ed.). 1990. *Second language writing: Research insights for the classroom.* New York: Cambridge University Press.

Kroll, B. (forthcoming). *In teachers' hands: A manual for the ESL writing teacher.*

Leki, I. 1990. Coaching from the margins: Issues in written response. In B. Kroll (ed.) *Second language writing: Research insights for the classroom.* New York: Cambridge University Press, 57–68.

Leki, I. 1991. Twenty-five years of contrastive rhetoric: Text analysis and writing pedagogies. *TESOL Quarterly* 25: 123–143.

Leki, I. 1992. *Understanding ESL writers: A guide for teachers.* Portsmouth, NH: Boynton/Cook.

Leki, I., and J. Carson. 1997. "Completely different worlds": EAP and the writing experiences of ESL students in university courses. *TESOL Quarterly* 31: 39–69.

Masters, E. L. 1920. *Spoon River Anthology.* New York: The Macmillan Company.

Maybin, J., and N. Mercer. 1996. *Using English: From conversation to canon.* London: Routledge.

McKay, S. (ed.). 1984. *Composing in a second language.* Rowley, MA: Newbury House.

Meyer, E., and L. Z. Smith. 1987. *The practical tutor.* New York: Oxford University Press.

Mittan, R. 1989. The peer review process: Harnessing students' communicative power. In D. Johnson and D. Roen (eds.), *Richness in writing: Empowering ESL students.* New York: Longman.

Morris, M. 1988. *Nothing to declare: Memoirs of a woman traveling alone.* New York: Penguin.

Mukherjee, B. 1989. *Jasmine.* New York: Fawcett Crest.

Murray, D. M. 1984. The listening eye: Reflections on the writing conference. In R.L. Graves (ed.), *Rhetoric and composition.* Upper Montclair,NJ: Boynton/Cook Publishers, 263-268. Also appears 1977 in *College English* 39: 449-461.

Peitzman, F., and G. Gadda. 1994. *With different eyes: Insights into teaching language minority students across the disciplines.* Reading, MA: Addison-Wesley.

Purves, A. C. (ed.). 1988. *Writing across languages and cultures: Issues in contrastive rhetoric.* Newbury Park, CA: Sage.

Raimes, A. 1991. Out of the woods: Emerging tradition in the teaching of writing. *TESOL Quarterly* 25: 407–430.

Reid, J. M. 1993. *Teaching ESL writing.* Englewood Cliffs, N.J.: Prentice-Hall.

Roen, D. H. 1989. Developing effective assignments for second language writers. In D. Johnson and D. Roen (eds.), *Richness in writing: Empowering ESL students.* New York: Longman, 193–206.

Rose, M. 1980. Rigid rules, inflexible plans, and the stifling of language: A cognitivist analysis of writer's block. *College Composition and Communication* 31: 389.

Rose, M. 1989. *Lives on the boundary: The struggles and achievements of America's underprepared.* New York: Penguin.

Rose, M. 1995. *Possible lives: The promise of public education in America.* Boston: Houghton Mifflin.

Schofield, J. W. 1995. *Computers and classroom culture.* Cambridge: Cambridge, UK: University Press.

Scott, V. M. 1996. *Rethinking foreign language writing.* Boston: Heinle & Heinle.

Severino, C., J. C. Guerra, and J. E. Butler (eds.). 1997. *Writing in multicultural settings.* New York: Modern Language Association.

Shih, M. 1986. Content-based approaches to teaching academic writing. *TESOL Quarterly* 20: 617–648.

Snow, M. A., and D. M. Brinton (eds.). 1997. *The content-based classroom: Perspectives on integrating language and content.* White Plains, NY: Longman.

Sommers, N. 1984. Responding to student writing. In S. McKay (ed.), *Composing in a Second Language.* Rowley, MA: Newbury House, 160-169.

Stanley, J. 1992. Coaching student writers to be effective peer evaluators. *Journal of second language Writing* 1: 217–233.

Steinbeck, J. 1945. *Cannery row.* New York: Viking Press.

Swales, J. 1990. *Genre analysis: English in academic and research settings.* Cambridge, UK: Cambridge University Press.

Ventola, E., and A. Mauranen (eds.). 1996. *Academic writing: Intercultural and textual issues.* Amsterdam: Johan Benjamins.

Warschauer, M. 1996. *E-mail for English teaching: Bringing the Internet and computer learning networks into the language classroom.* Alexandria, VA: Teachers of English to Speakers of Other Languages, Inc.

Writers at work: The Paris Review interviews. Series since 1983. New York: Penguin.

Zamel, V. 1982. Writing: The process of discovering meaning. *TESOL Quarterly* 16: 195–209.